I0503739

Horses Jumbo Adult Coloring Book Horses and Ponies Grazing and Racing Color By Number

By Color Questopia

Thank you
for your purchase!

**Claim your FREE digital copy of our
Highlight Reel Color By Number Book:**

Check out our website: colorquestopia.com

**Join our Facebook group:
facebook.com/colorquestopia**

Follow us on Instagram: @colorquestopia

**Did you enjoy this book?
Please leave us a review!**

https://geni.us/cqreview

Color By Number Tips

1. **Relax and have fun**
   Let your cares slip away as you color the images. Take your time. Coloring is a meditative activity and there's no wrong way to do it. Feel free to color as you listen to music, watch TV, lounge in bed- do whatever relaxes you most! You can also color while you're out and about- on the train or at a cafe- take the book with you anywhere you go. Coloring is therapeutic and is great for stress relief and relaxation!

2. **Colors corresponding to each number are shown on the back cover of the book**
   Each number corresponds to a color shown on the back of the book. You can match the color as closely as you like- but feel free to change the color or the shade if you don't have the exact color match- that's totally fine. Although this is a color by number book, it's completely okay to get creative and color the images with whichever colors you like and have. The numbers are there to be a guide and to allow you to color without having to focus your energy on choosing colors.

3. **Choose your coloring tools**
   Everyone has their favorite coloring markers, crayons, pencils, pens- even paints! Feel free to color with any tool that you like! If you choose markers or paints, we recommend putting a blank sheet of paper or cardboard behind each image, so that your colors don't run onto the next image.

   Enjoy!

1. Black

2. Sky blue

3. blue

4. Medium Blue

5. Light blue

6. Dark blue

7. Navy Blue

8. Brown

9. Dark browm

10. Light browm

11. Dark Red

12. Orange

13. Yellow

14. Gray

15. Dark Gray

16. Light Yellow

17. Light green

18. green

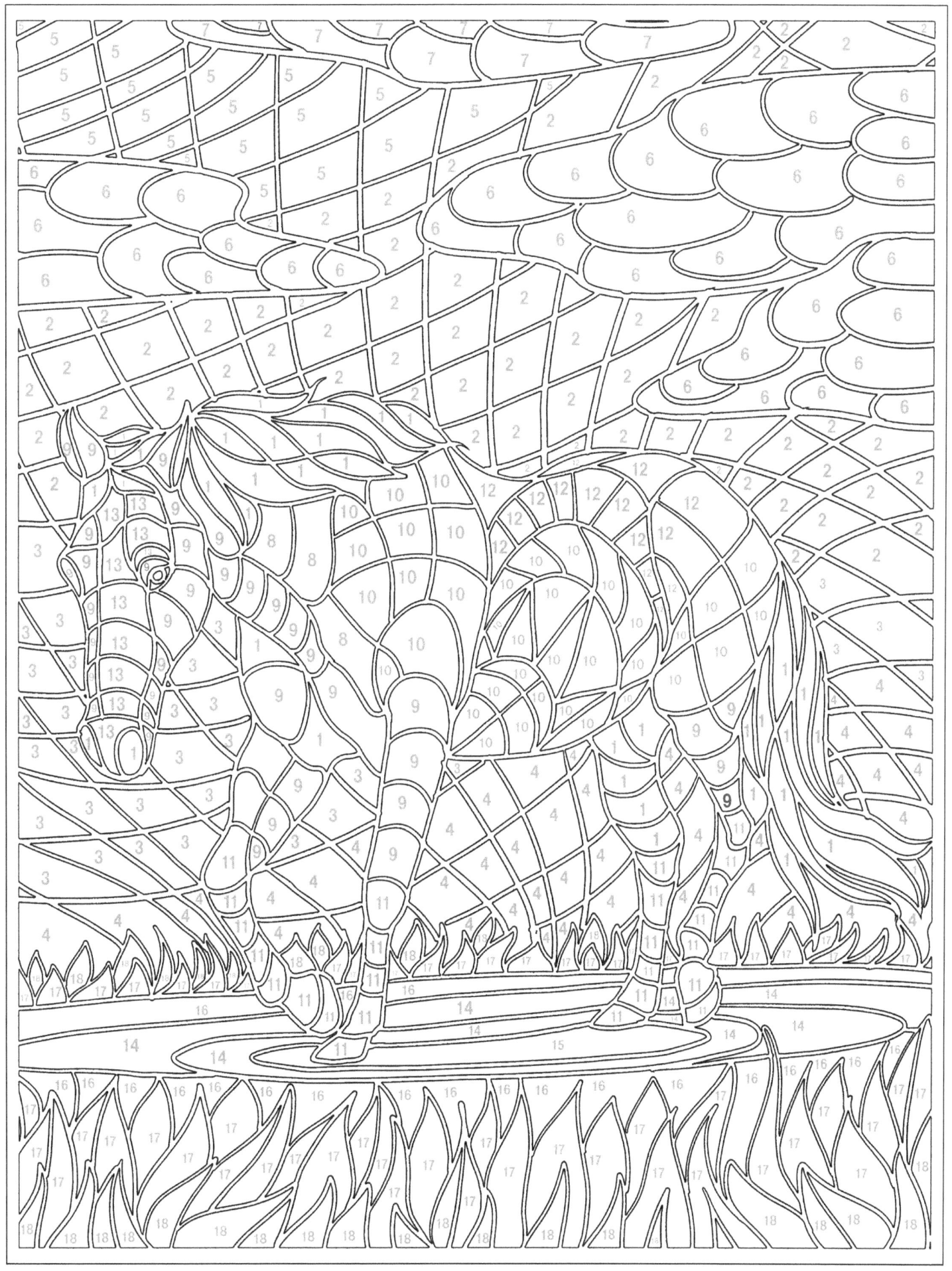

1. Dark brown

2. Dark Orange

3. Brown

4. Red

5. Medium Brown

6. Dark Orange

7. Orange

8. White

9. Light brown

10. Light Gray

11. Light Orange

12. Dark Yellow

13. Black

14. Army green

15. Light Red

16. Dark Red

17. Sky blue

18. Blue

19. Dark blue

20. Light blue

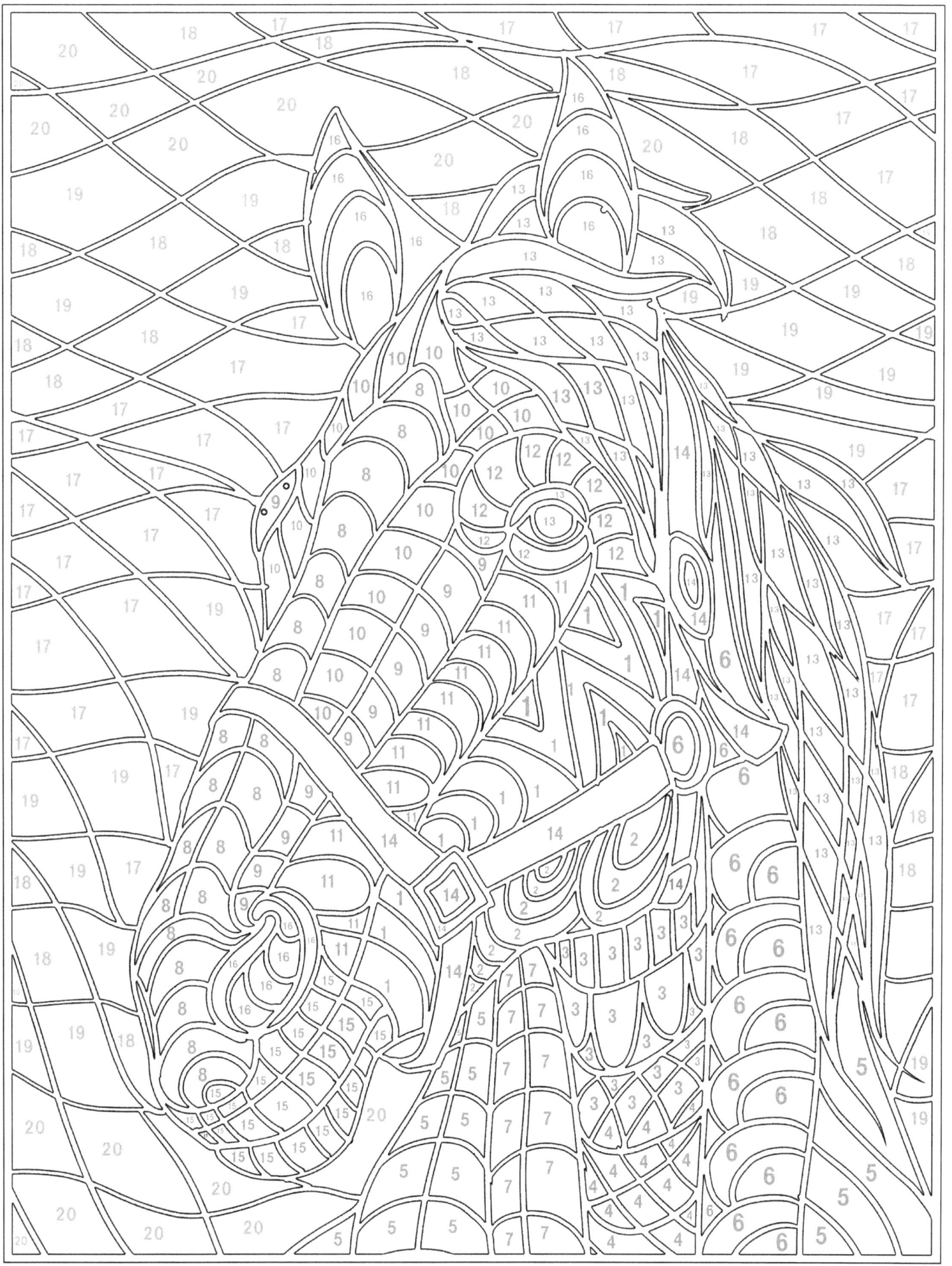

1. Brown

2. Light Brown

3. Dark Brown

4. White

5. Black

6. Light Orange

7. Orange

8. Dark Orange

9. Dark Gray

10. Gray

11. Light Gray

12. Light Green

13. Neon Green

14. Army Green

15. Sky blue

16. Dark Blue

17. Light Blue

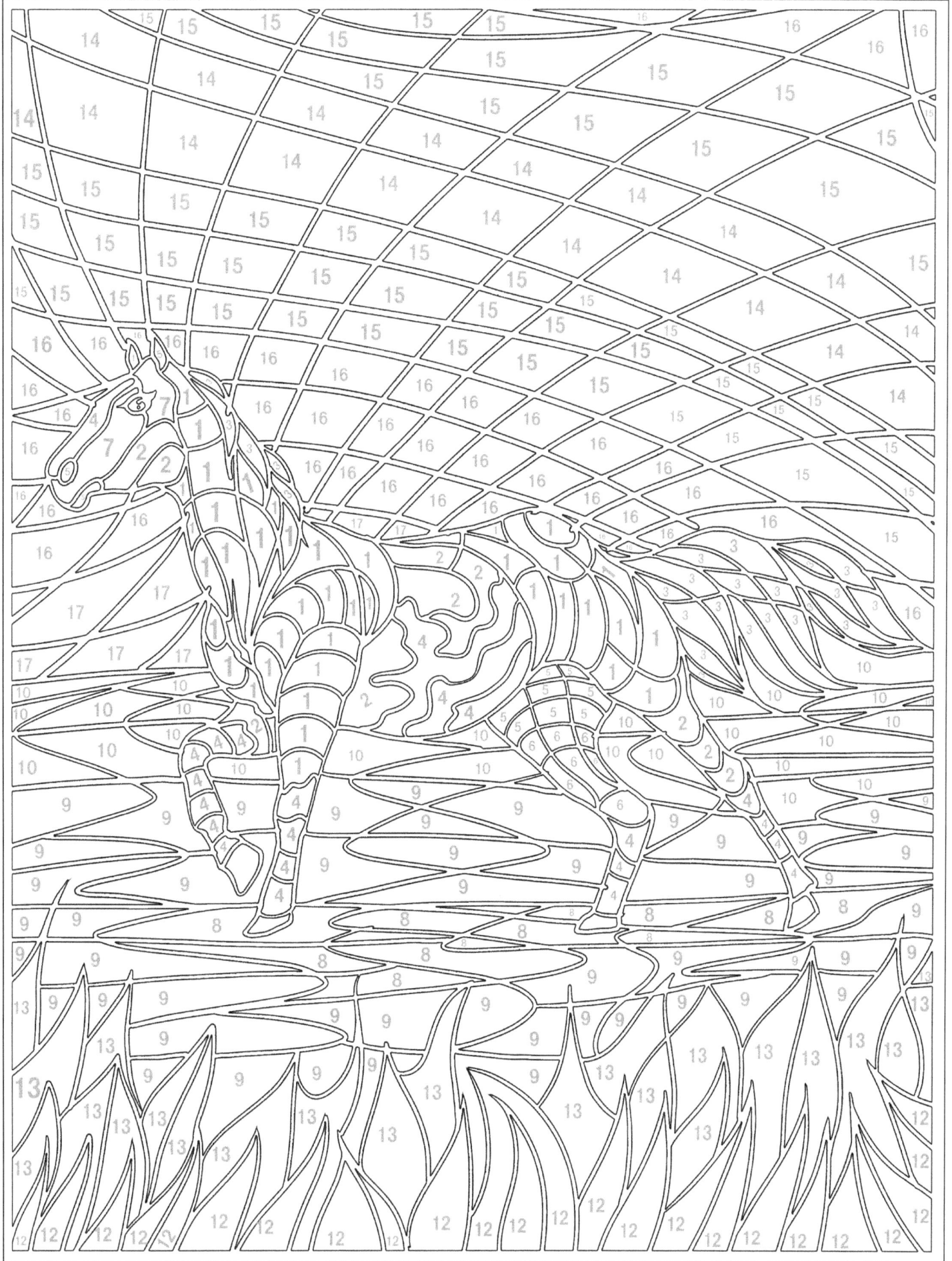

1. Dark Brown

2. Light Orange

3. Light Brown

4. Orange

5. Dark Orange

6. White

7. Brown

8. Dark Gray

9. Dark Violet

10. Yellow

11. Dark Yellow

12. Pink

13. Black

14. Red

15. Light Gray

16. Gray

17. Blue

18. Dark Blue

19. Medium Blue

20. violet

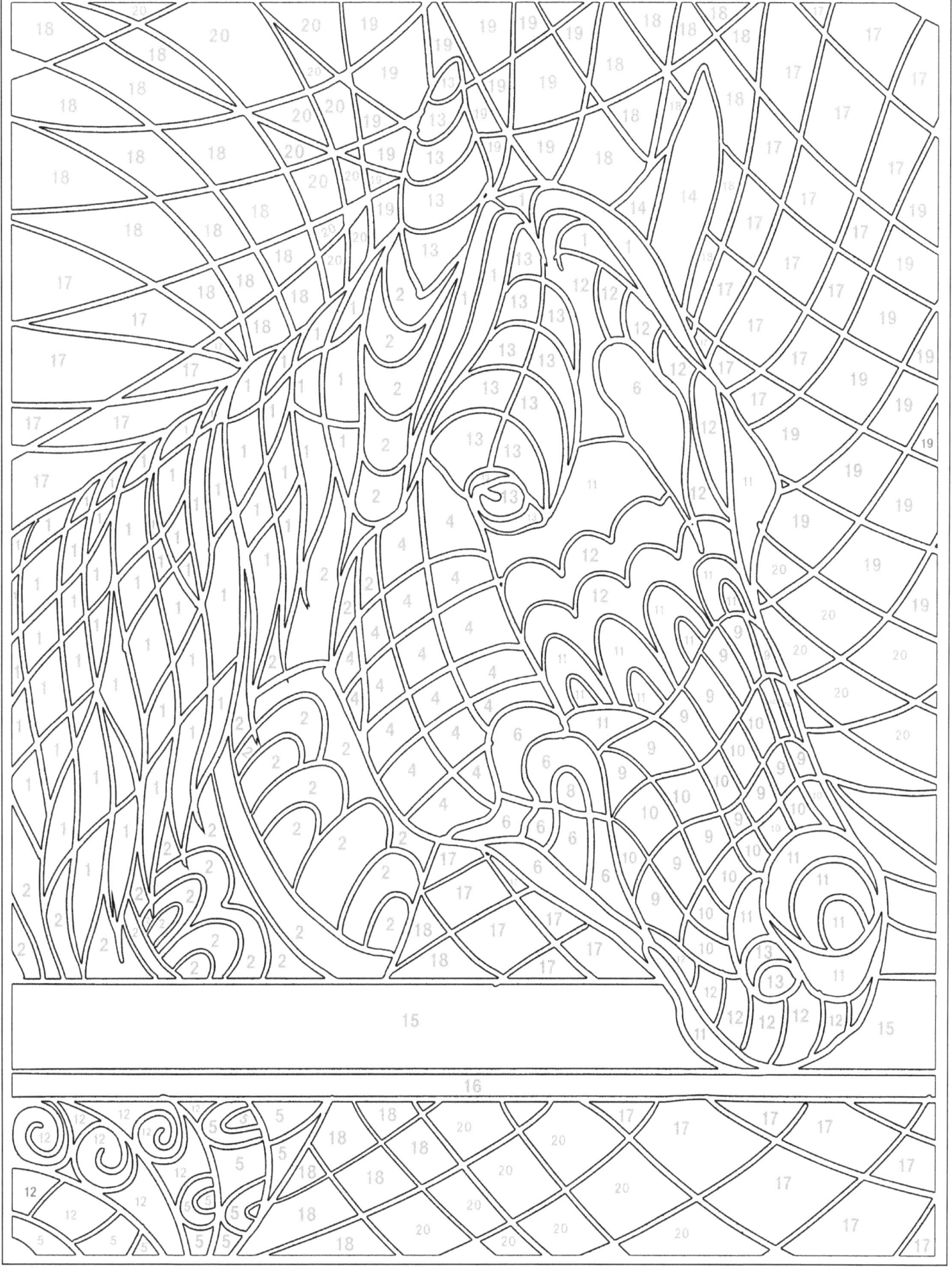

1. Violet

2. Dark violet

3. Soft violet

4. Brown

5. Gray

6. Dark Brown

7. Light Red

8. Pink

9. Light Brown

10. Medium Gray

11. Black

12. Red

13. Medium Green

14. Army green

15. Light green

16. green

17. Dark Green

18. Light Yellow

19. Neon Green

20. White

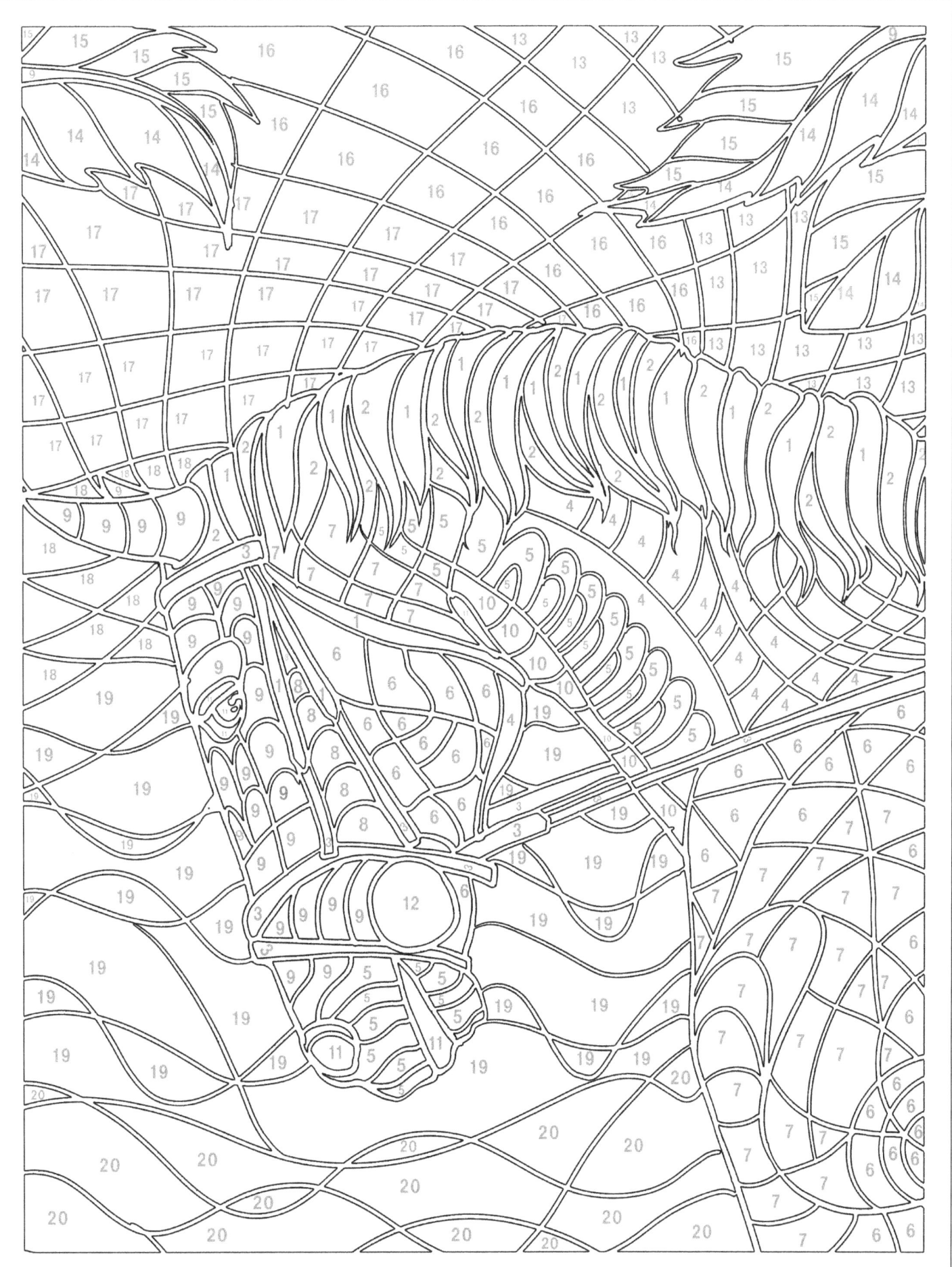

1. Light brown
2. brown
3. Dark Brown
4. Black
5. Dark Violet
6. Orange
7. Light Orange
8. Dark Orange
9. Orange
10. Medium Red
11. Dark Red
12. Light Yellow
13. Yellow
14. Dark Yellow
15. Green
16. Light green
17. Medium Gray
18. Gray
19. Sky blue
20. Blue
21. White

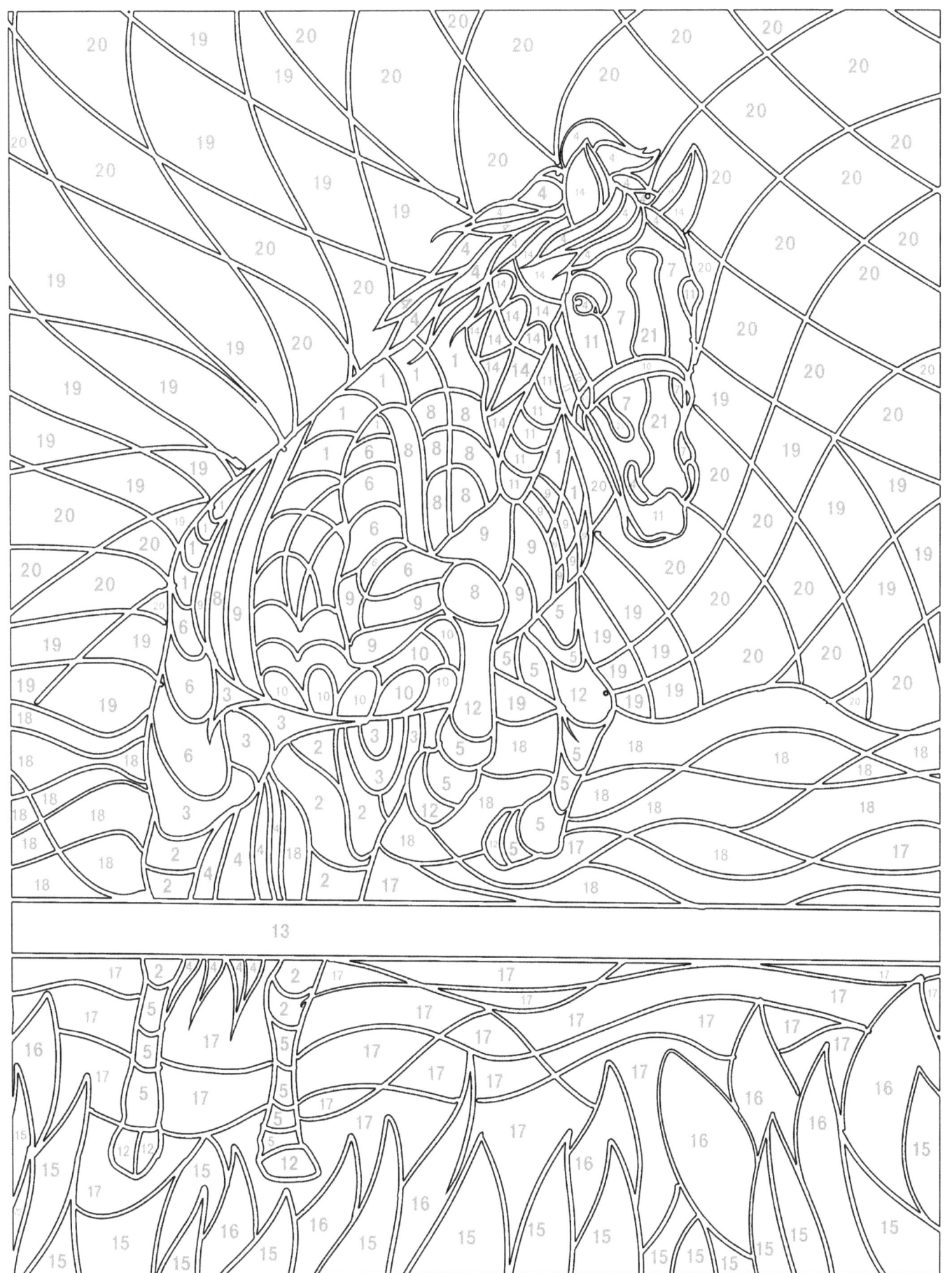

1. Orange

2. Light Orange

3. Dark orange

4. Brown

5. Dark Red

6. Light brown

7. Black

8. Light Yellow

9. Gray

10. Light Gray

11. Dark brown

12. Yellow

13. red

14. Pink

15. Light Pink

16. Deep Blue

17. Blue

18. Light Blue

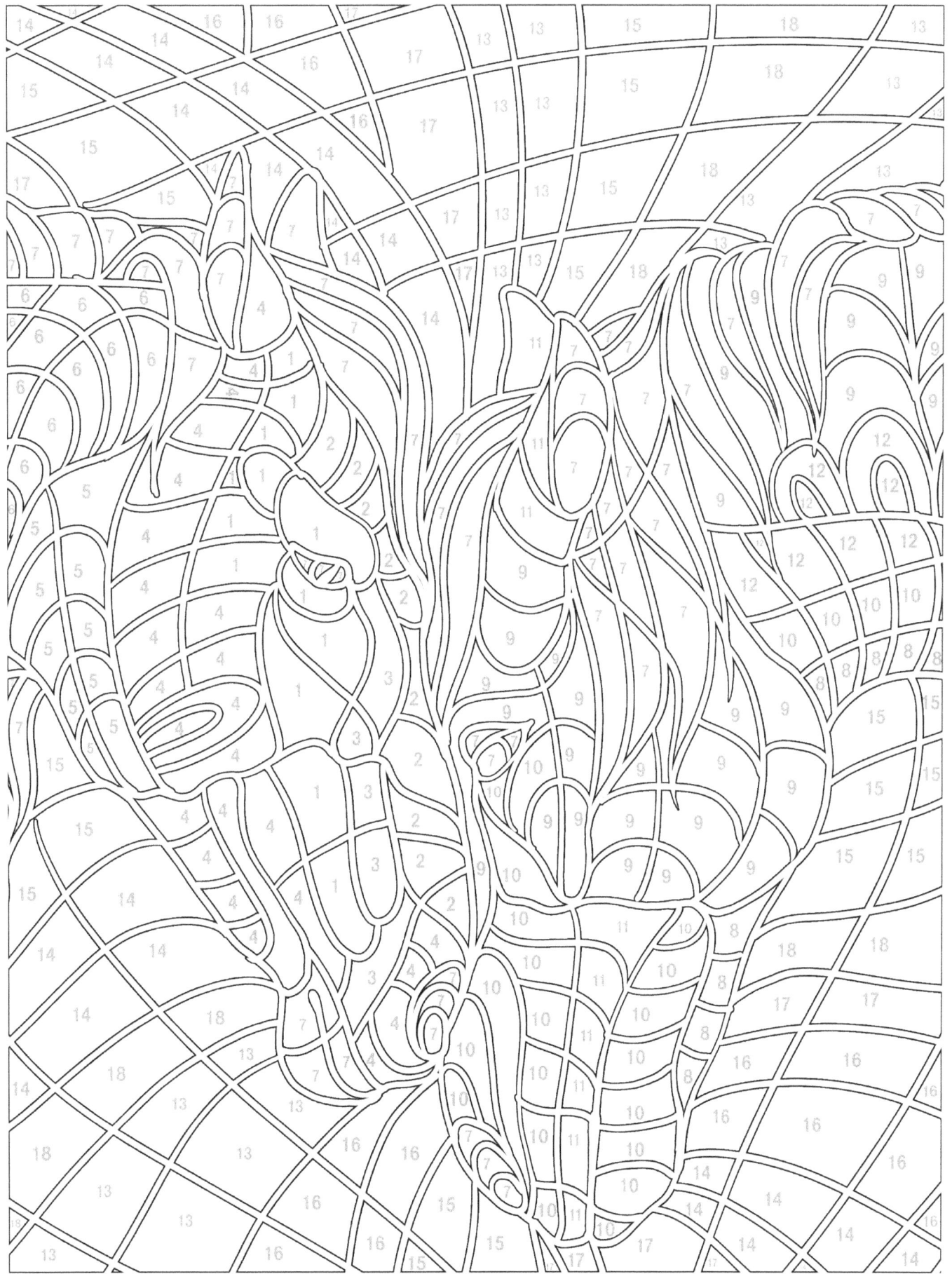

1. Black
2. Dark Brown
3. Light Gray
4. Brown
5. Light Red
6. Light Brown
7. Dark Orange
8. Red
9. Gray
10. Dark Gray
11. Orange
12. Light Green
13. Green
14. Light Blue
15. Blue
16. Sky Blue
17. Baby blue
18. Medium Blue
19. Violet
20. Light Violet

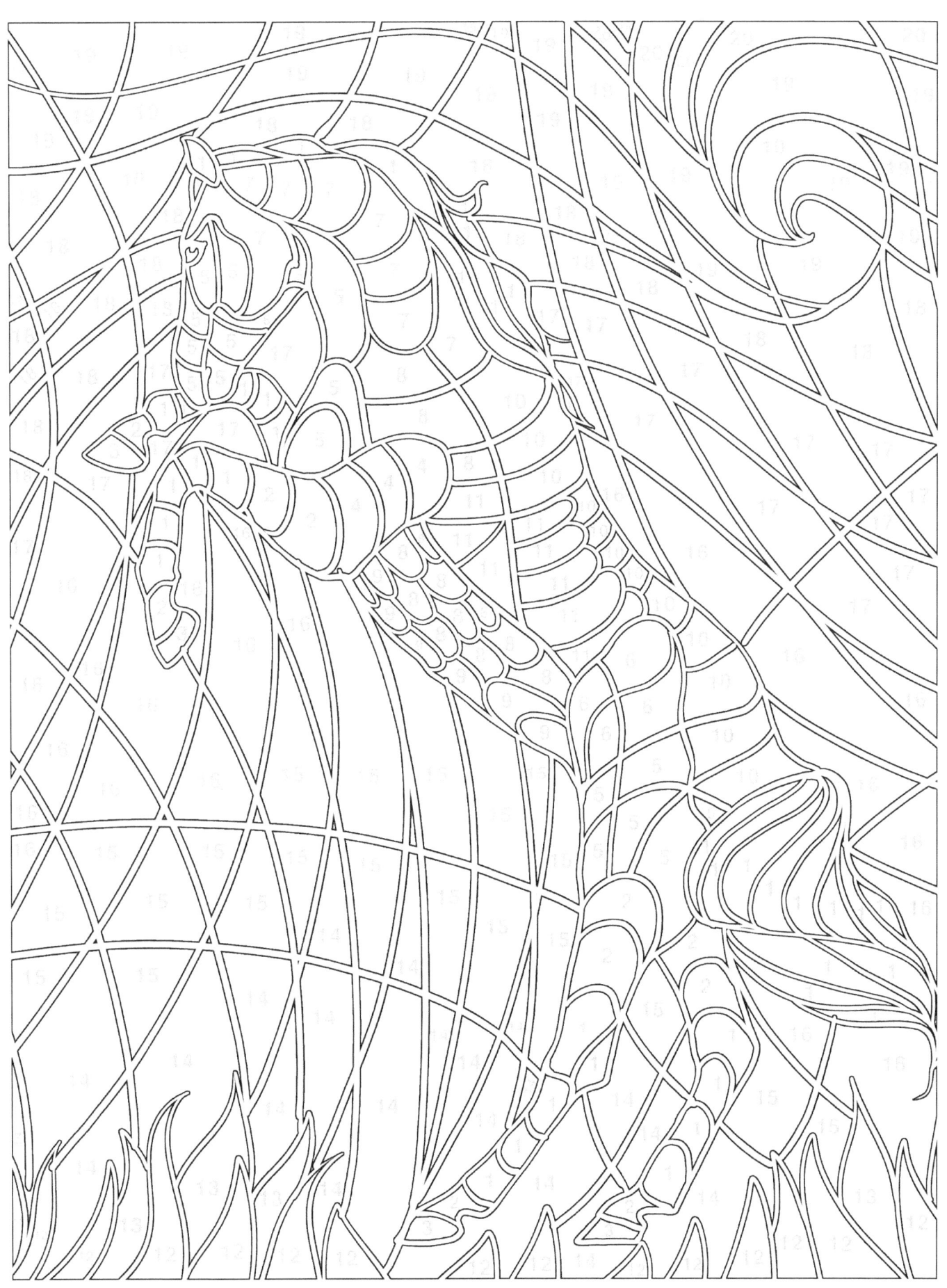

1. Dark Red

2. Dark Brown

3. Medium Gray

4. Light Brown

5. Light Red

6. Dark Orange

7. Brown

8. Orange

9. Light Orange

10. Medium Red

11. Gray

12. Light Violet

13. Yellow

14. Army Green

15. Green

16. Light Green

17. Light Yellow

18. Beige

19. Sky Blue

20. Medium Blue

21. Navy Blue

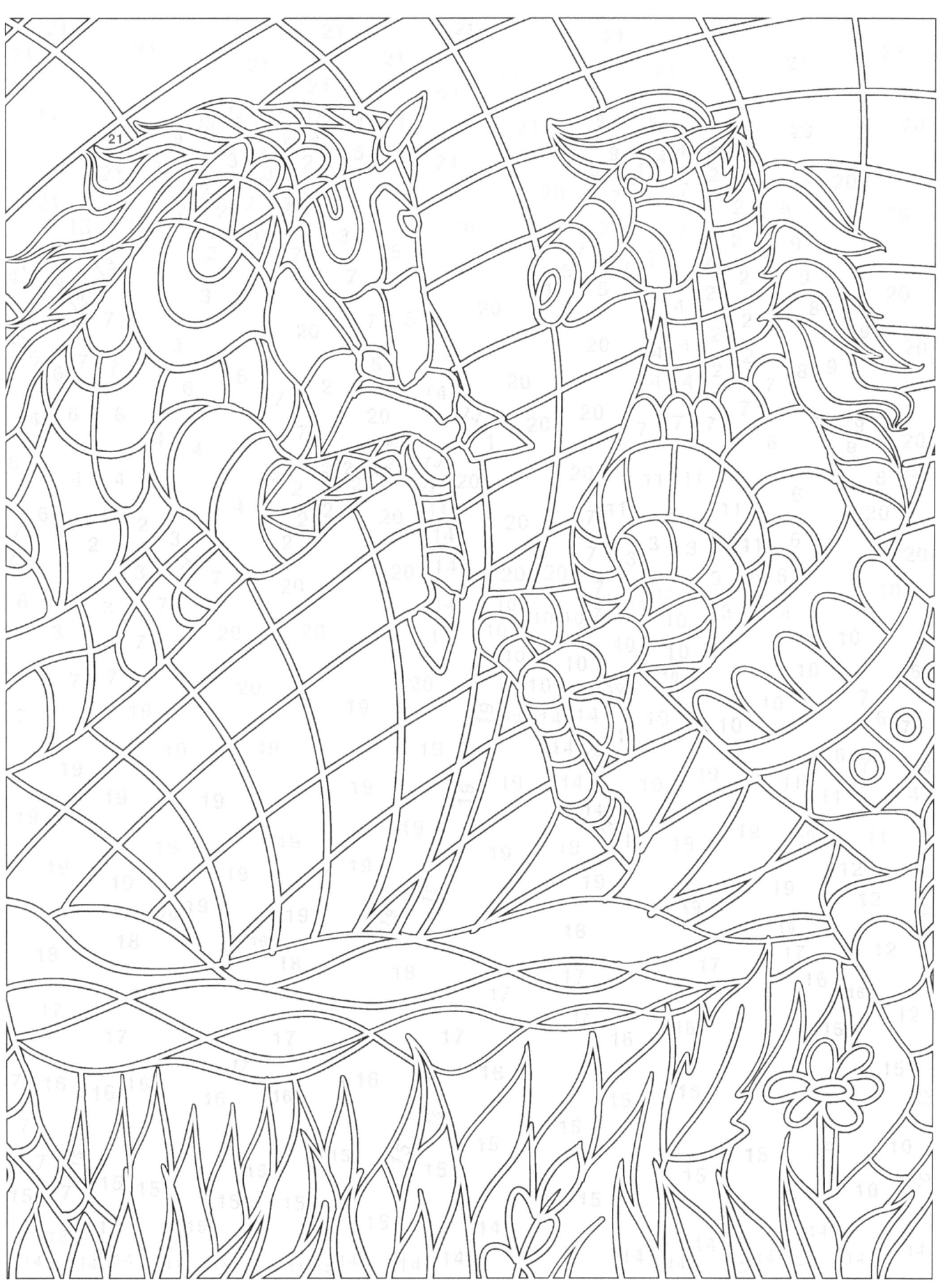

1. Dark Red

2. Brown

3. Dark Orange

4. Dark Brown

5. Orange

6. Light Gray

7. Light Red

8. Light Brown

9. Light Orange

10. Medium Brown

11. Yellow

12. Dark Gray

13. Light Gray

14. Light Orange

15. Blue

16. Sky Blue

17. Navy Blue

18. Light Blue

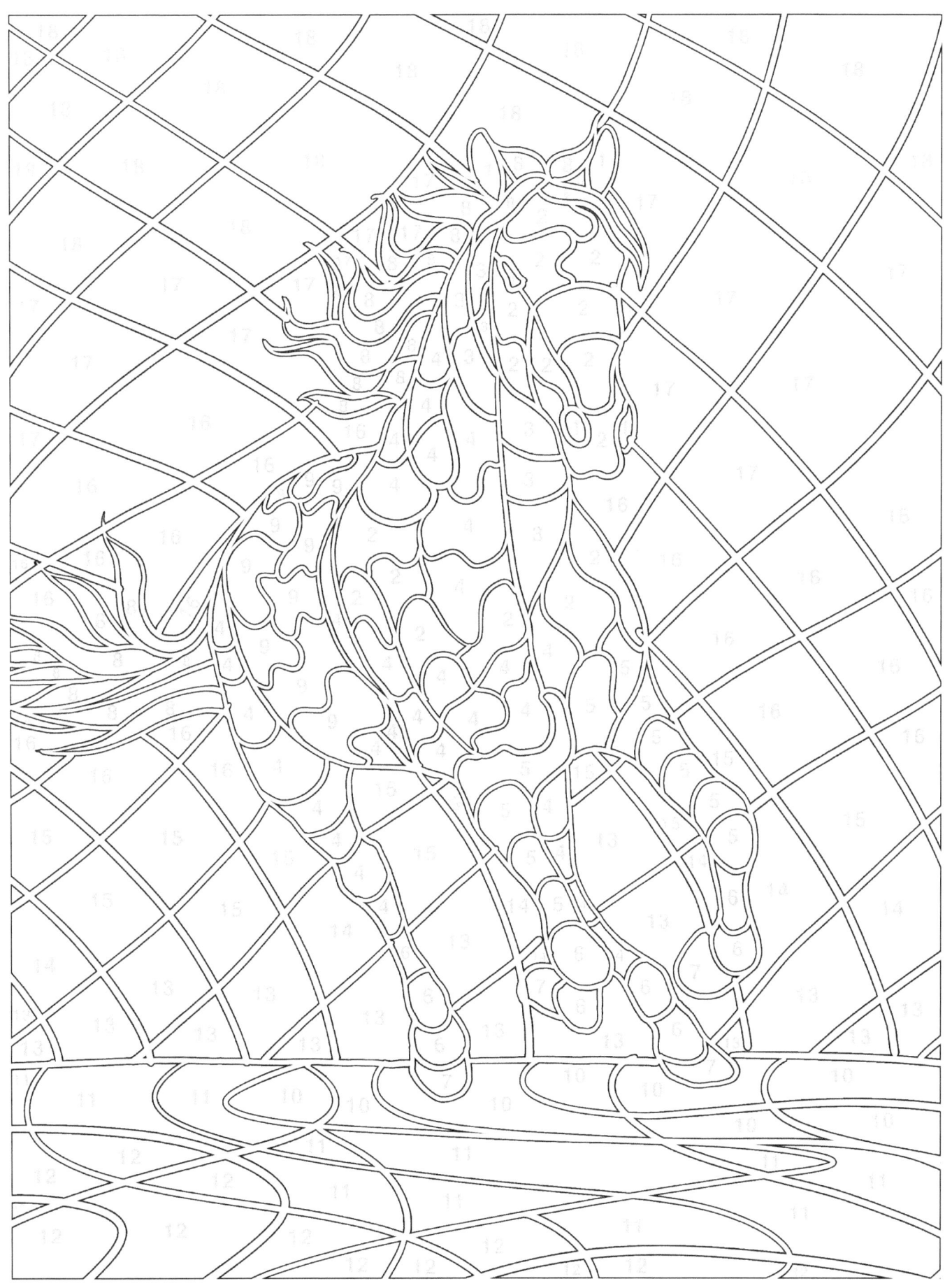

1. Black

2. Light chocolate

3. Dark Brown

4. Orange

5. Dark Orange

6. Light Pink

7. Light Orange

8. Dark Orange

9. Brown

10. Hot Pink

11. Dark Gray

12. Light Red

13. Bright Orange

14. Dark Red

15. Gray

16. Dark Violet

17. Dark Yellow

18. Peanut Brown

19. Light Brown

20. Red

21. Yellow

22. Beige

23. Medium Pink

24. Light Yellow

25. Light Green

26. Light Violet

27. Light Gray

28. Coffee

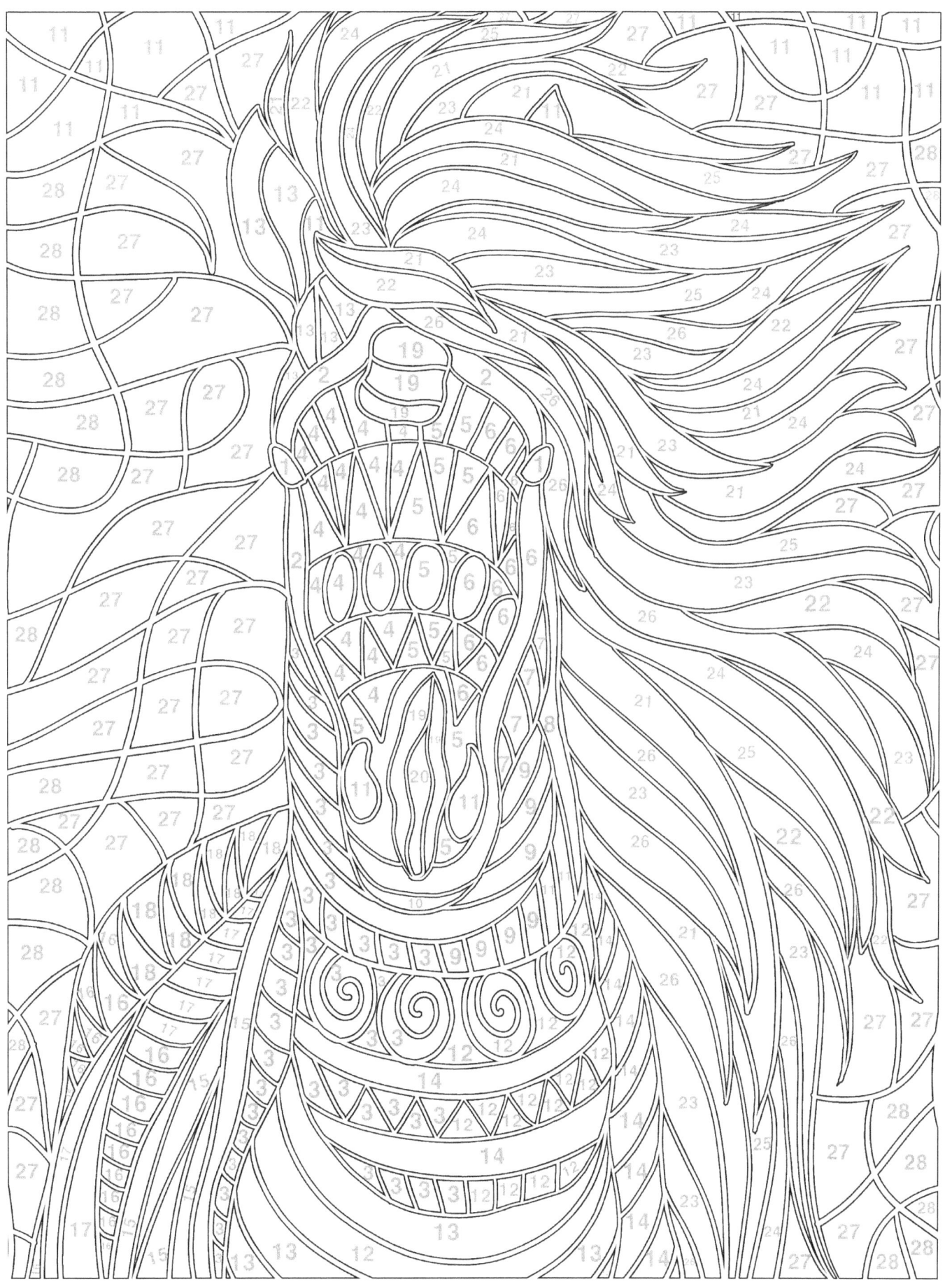

1. Black	16. Blue
2. White	17. Light Blue
3. Brown	18. Sky Blue
4. Dark Brown	19. Navy Blue
5. Dark Red	20. Medium Blue
6. Orange	
7. Dark Orange	
8. Light Brown	
9. Light Orange	
10. Army Green	
11. Light Green	
12. Green	
13. Medium Green	
14. Yellow	
15. Dark Green	

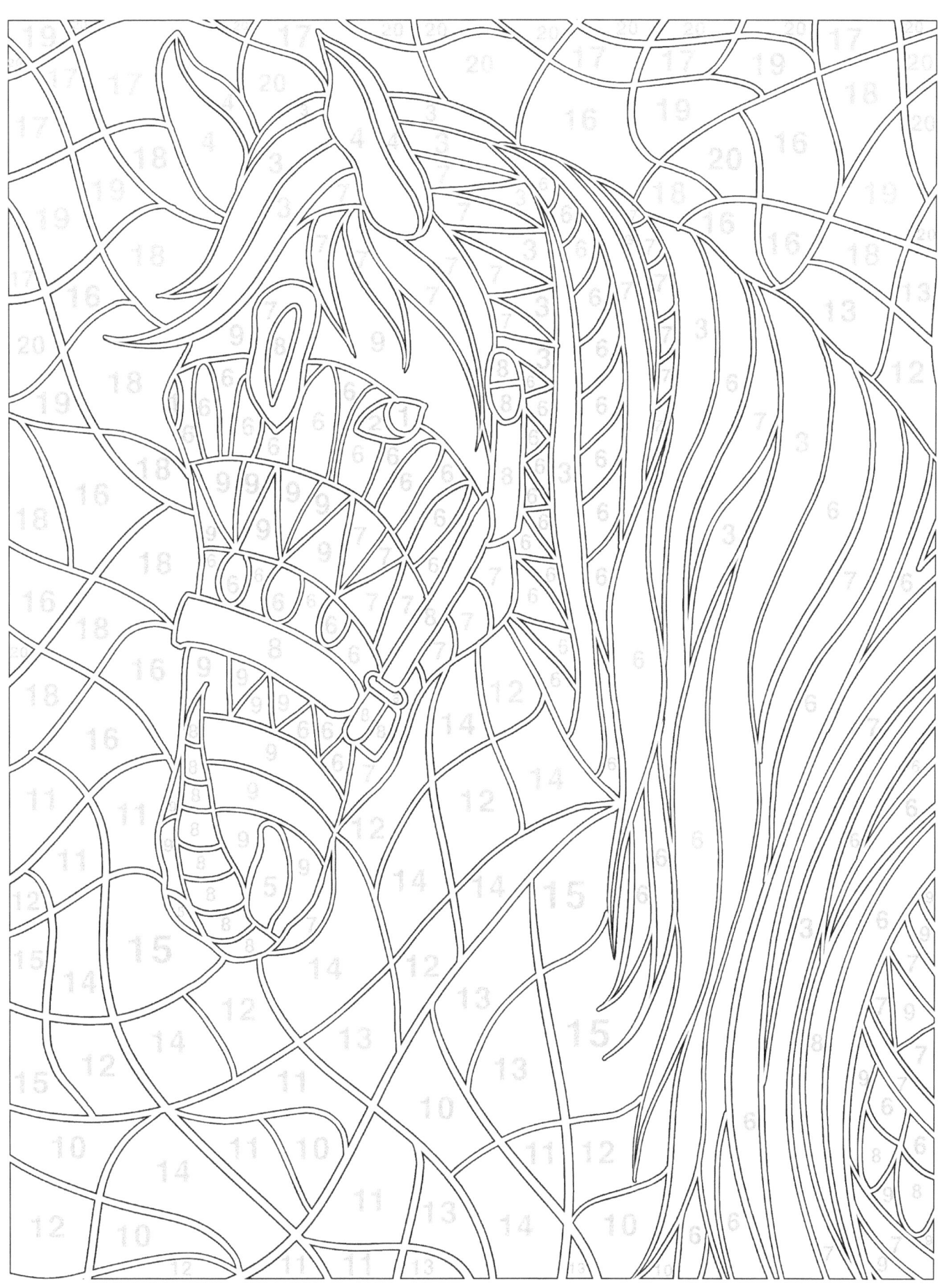

1. Black	16. Dark Brown
2. Light Red	17. Green
3. Bright Orange	18. Light Green
4. Light Orange	19. Medium Blue
5. Dark Red	20. Blue
6. Brown	21. Sky Blue
7. Light Brown	
8. Gray	
9. Dark Orange	
10. Orange	
11. Light Pink	
12. Medium Pink	
13. Yellow	
14. Red	
15. Medium Red	

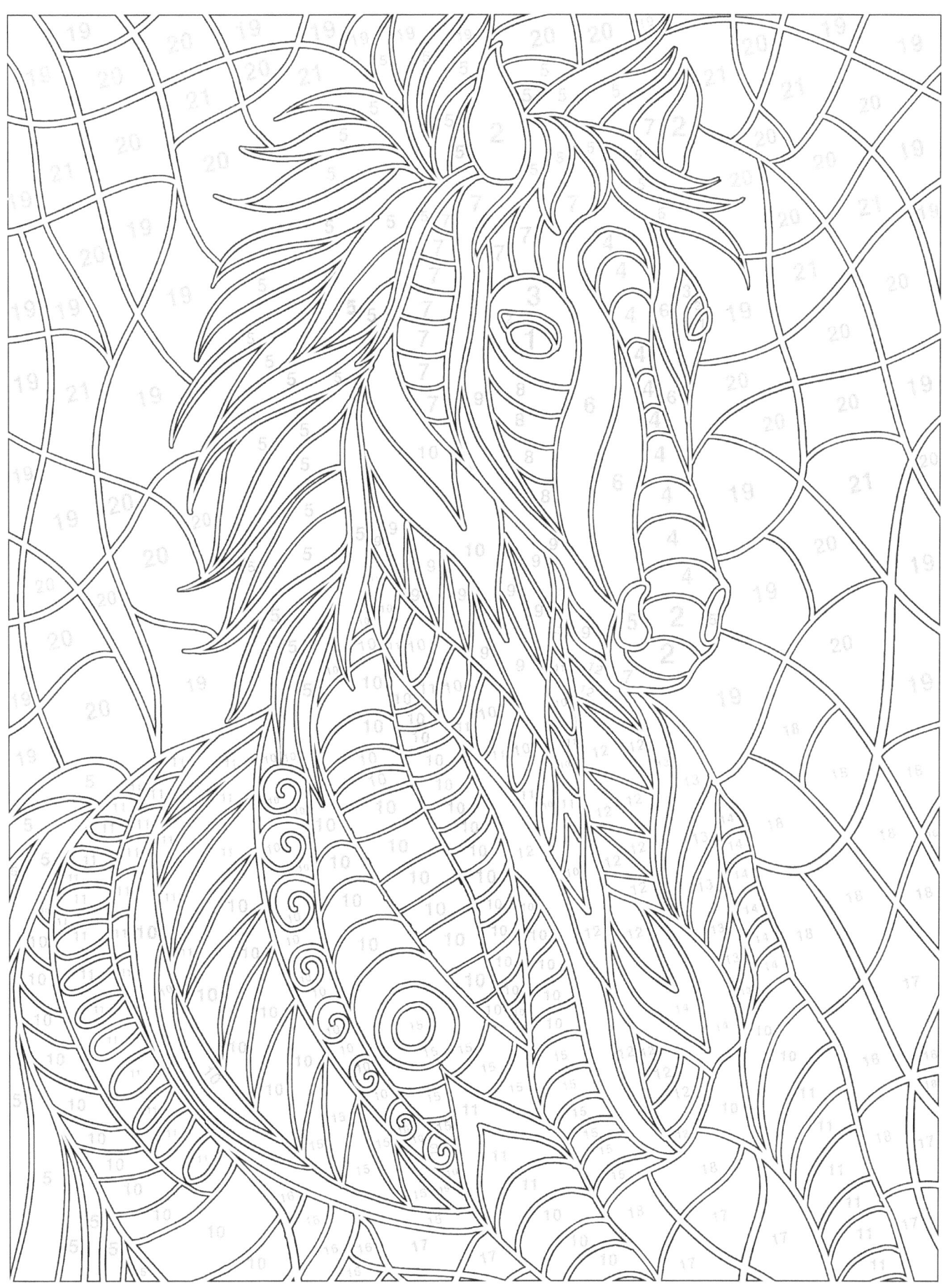

1. Black

2. Dark Brown

3. Dark Orange

4. Light Red

5. Beige

6. Dark Red

7. Brown

8. Soft Violet

9. Light Red

10. Army Green

11. Light Green

12. Yellow

13. Green

14. Light Brown

15. Neon Green

16. Light Yellow

17. Blue

18. Green

19. Medium Green

20. Dark Green

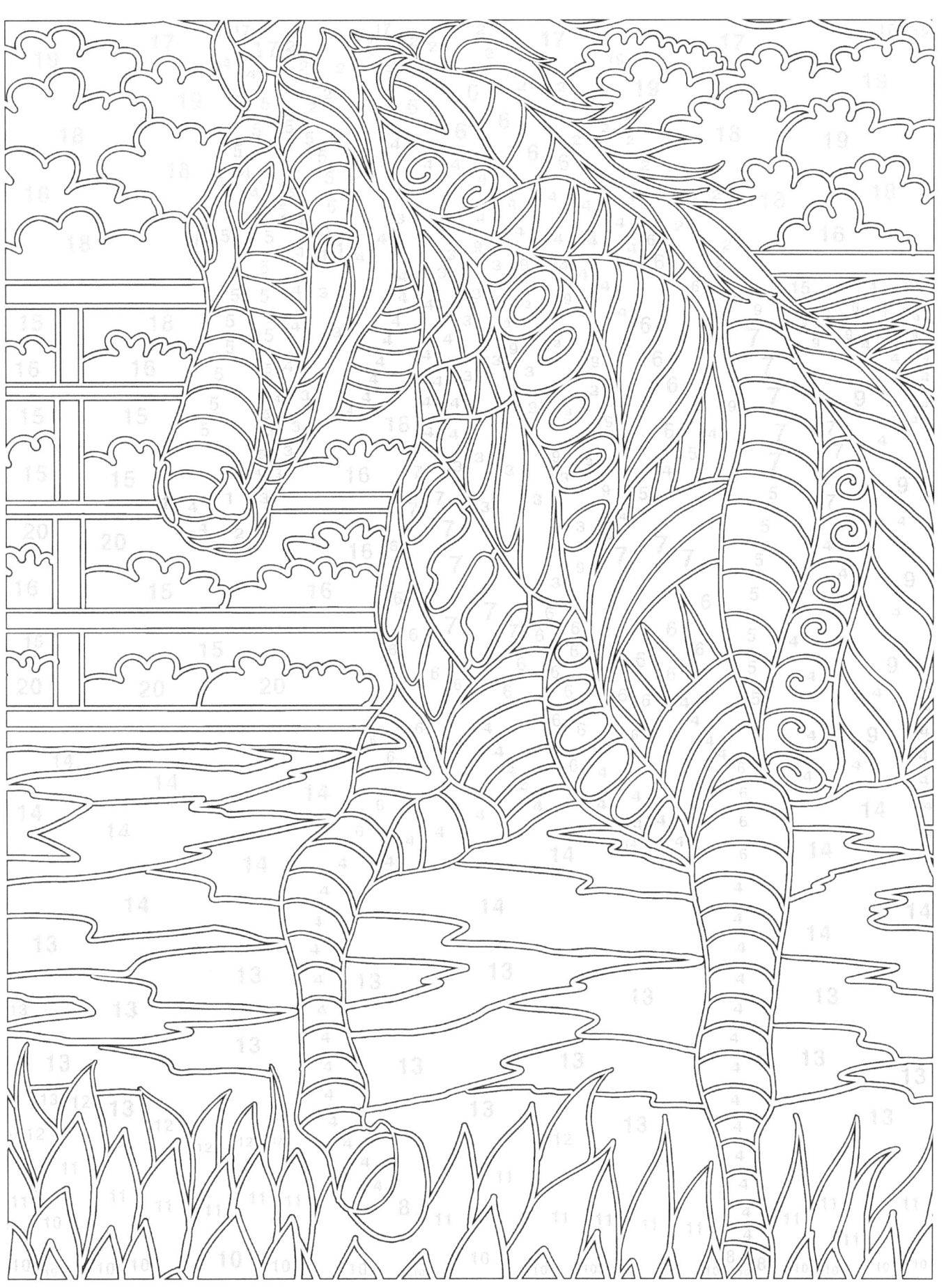

1. Black
2. Dark Brown
3. Light Orange
4. Light Yellow
5. Dark Red
6. Soft Violet
7. Light Brown
8. Orange
9. Yellow
10. Dark Orange
11. Bright Orange
12. Light Red
13. Dark Green
14. Green
15. Neon Green
16. Light Yellow
17. Sky Blue
18. Navy Blue
19. Light Blue
20. Medium Blue

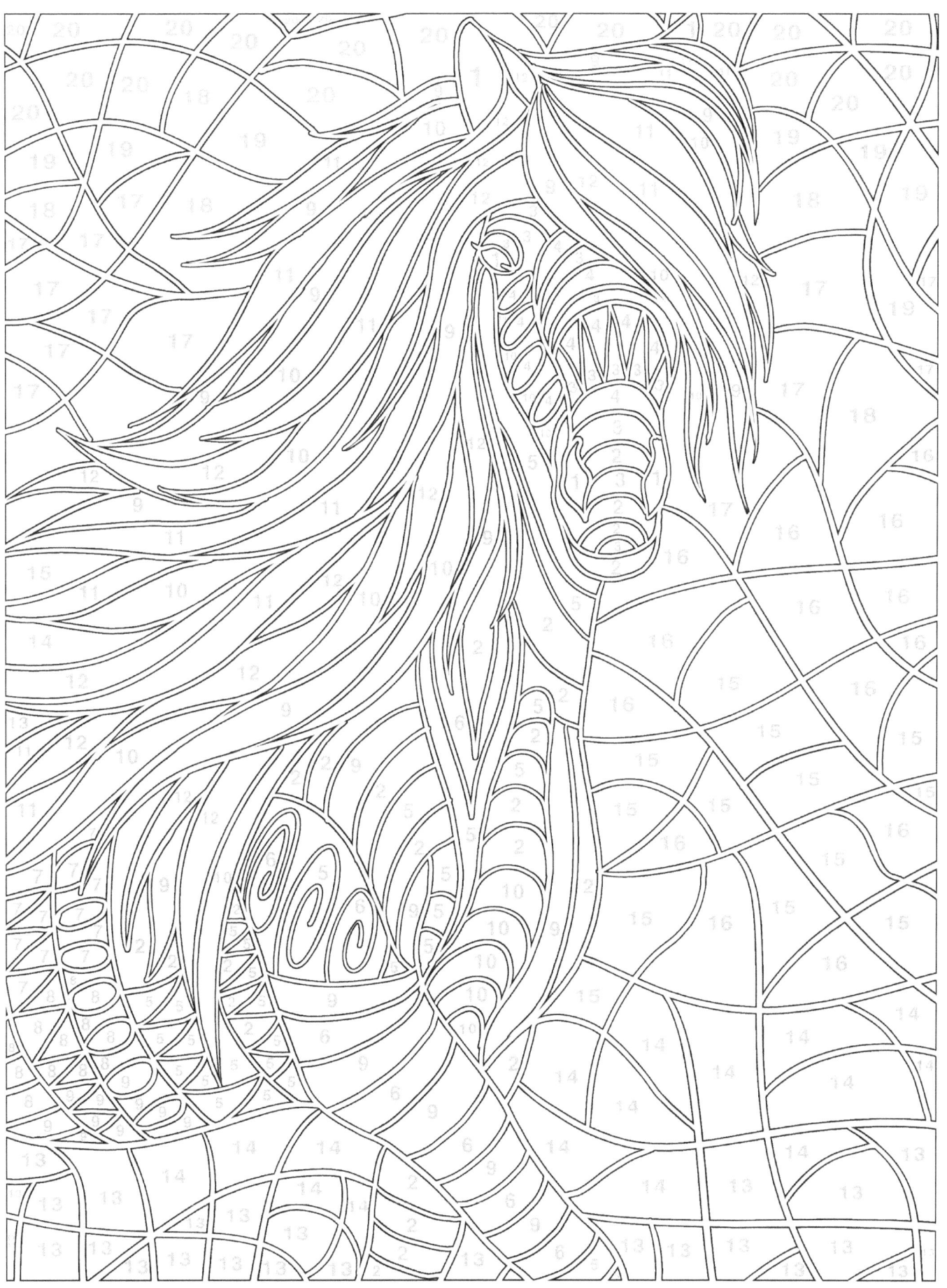

1. Yellow

2. Light Brown

3. Dark brown

4. Light Red

5. Brown

6. Dark Orange

7. Orange

8. Dark Red

9. Light Yellow

10. Yellow

11. White

12. Black

13. Light green

14. green

15. Army Green

16. Light blue

17. Navy Blue

18. Sky Blue

19. Dark blue

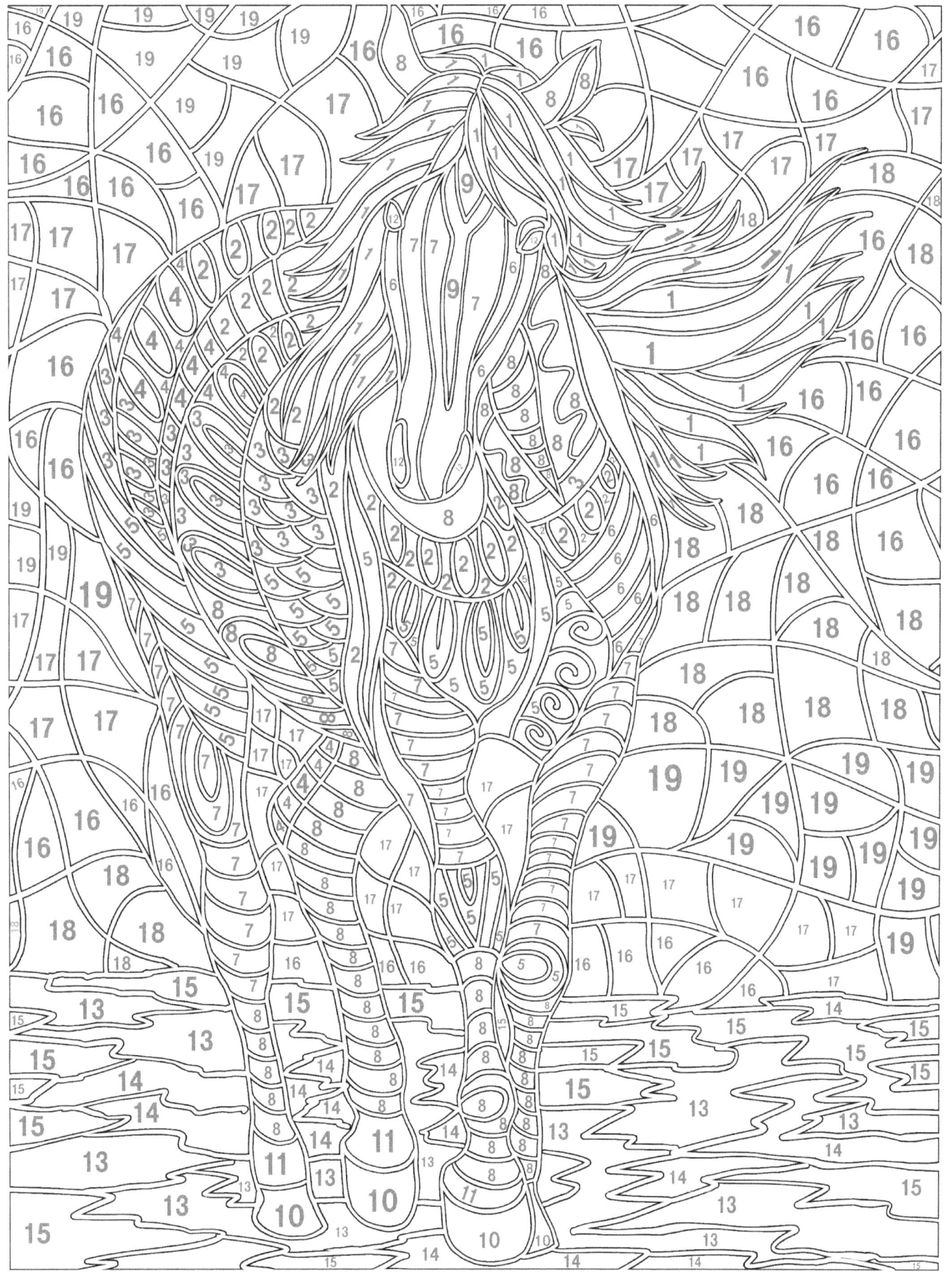

1. Black

2. Dark Brown

3. Light Brown

4. Light Orange

5. Orange

6. Light Gray

7. Yellow

8. Brown

9. Gray

10. Dark Orange

11. Hot Pink

12. Light Yellow

13. Light Pink

14. Light Red

15. Light Yellow

16. Yellow

17. Red Brown

18. Soft Violet

19. Dark Pink

20. Medium Purple

21. Dark Green

22. Army Green

23. Green

24. Light Green

25. Sky Blue

26. Blue

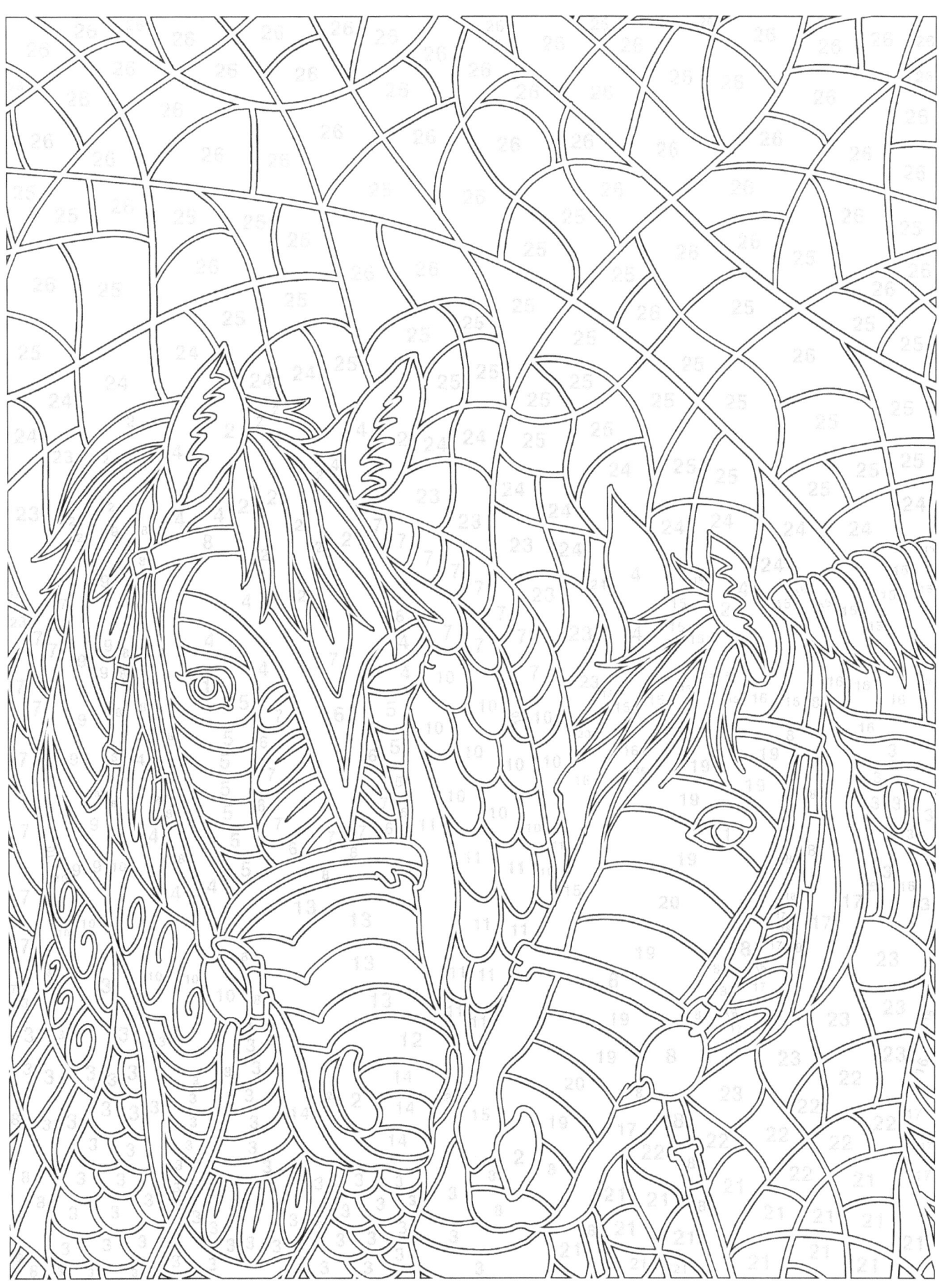

1. Black	16. Navy Blue
2. Dark Brown	17. Sky Blue
3. Red	18. Medium Blue
4. Light Brown	
5. Orange	
6. Light Pink	
7. Soft Violet	
8. Dark Orange	
9. Medium Red	
10. Dark Red	
11. Dark Green	
12. Green	
13. Light Green	
14. Neon Green	
15. Yellow	

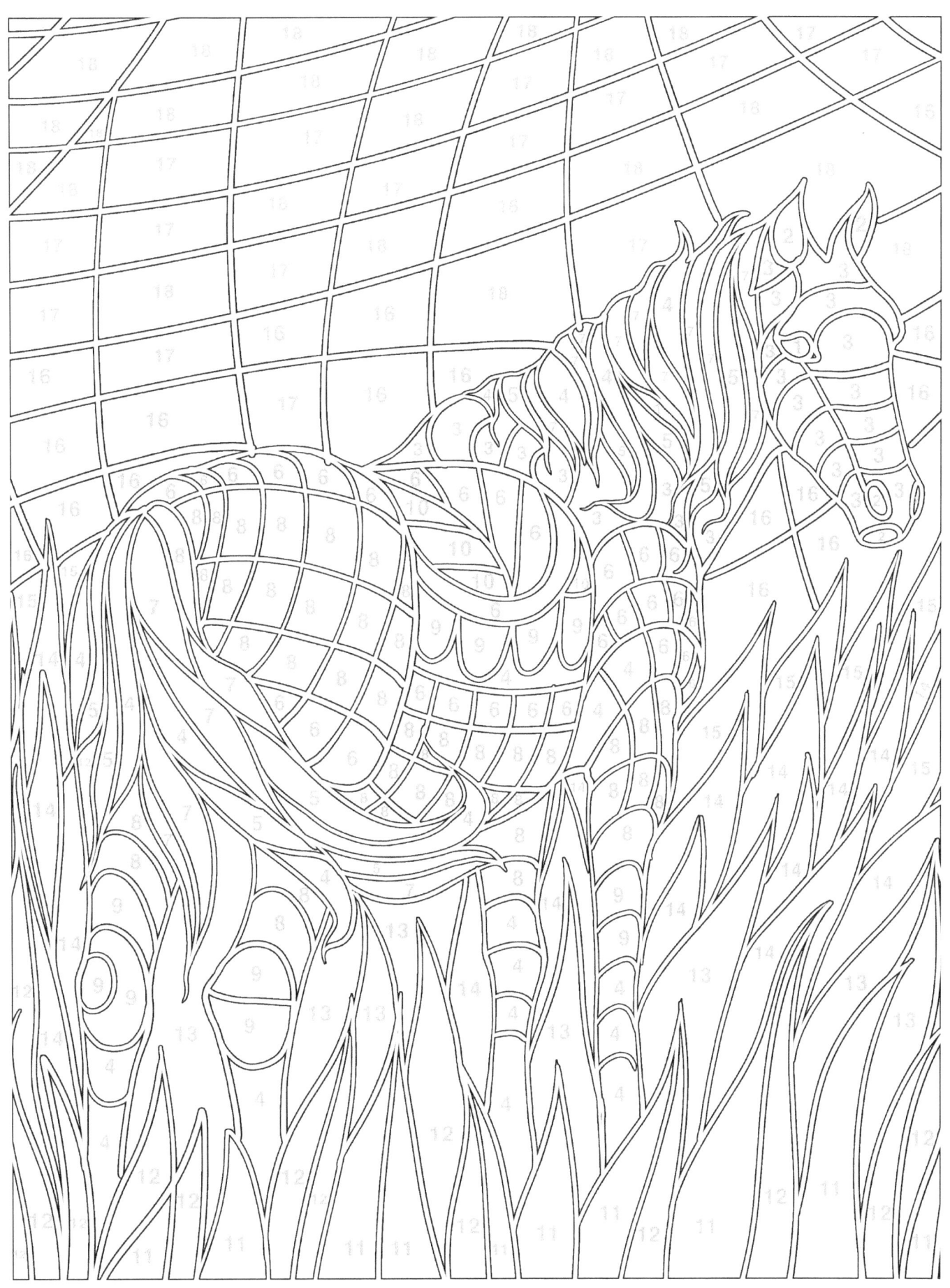

1. Black

2. Brown

3. Dark Brown

4. Light Brown

5. Red

6. Light Yellow

7. Dark Yellow

8. Dark Red

9. Gray

10. Light Gray

11. Medium Purple

12. Soft Violet

13. Dark Blue

14. Medium Green

15. Light Green

16. Deep Green

17. Dark Yellow

18. Yellow

19. Orange

20. Light Orange

21. Pink

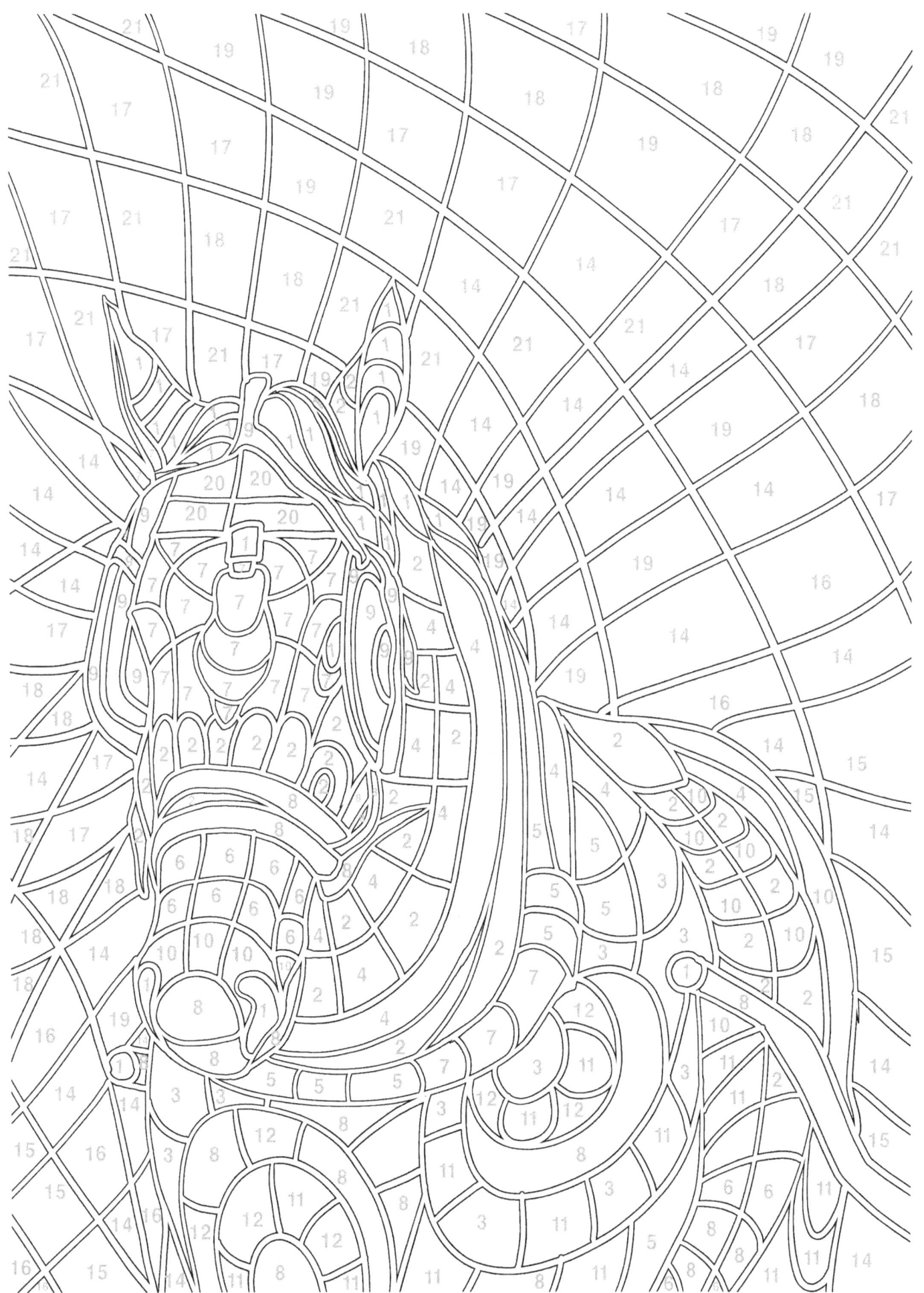

1. Black

2. Light Brown

3. Dark Red

4. Brown

5. Orange

6. Dark Orange

7. Soft Violet

8. Dark Brown

9. Light Red

10. Gray

11. Yellow

12. Dark Red

13. Light Gray

14. Army Green

15. Medium Green

16. Dark Green

17. Violet

18. Blue

19. Pink

20. Neon Green

21. Green

22. Light Green

23. Navy Blue

24. Medium Blue

25. Sky Blue

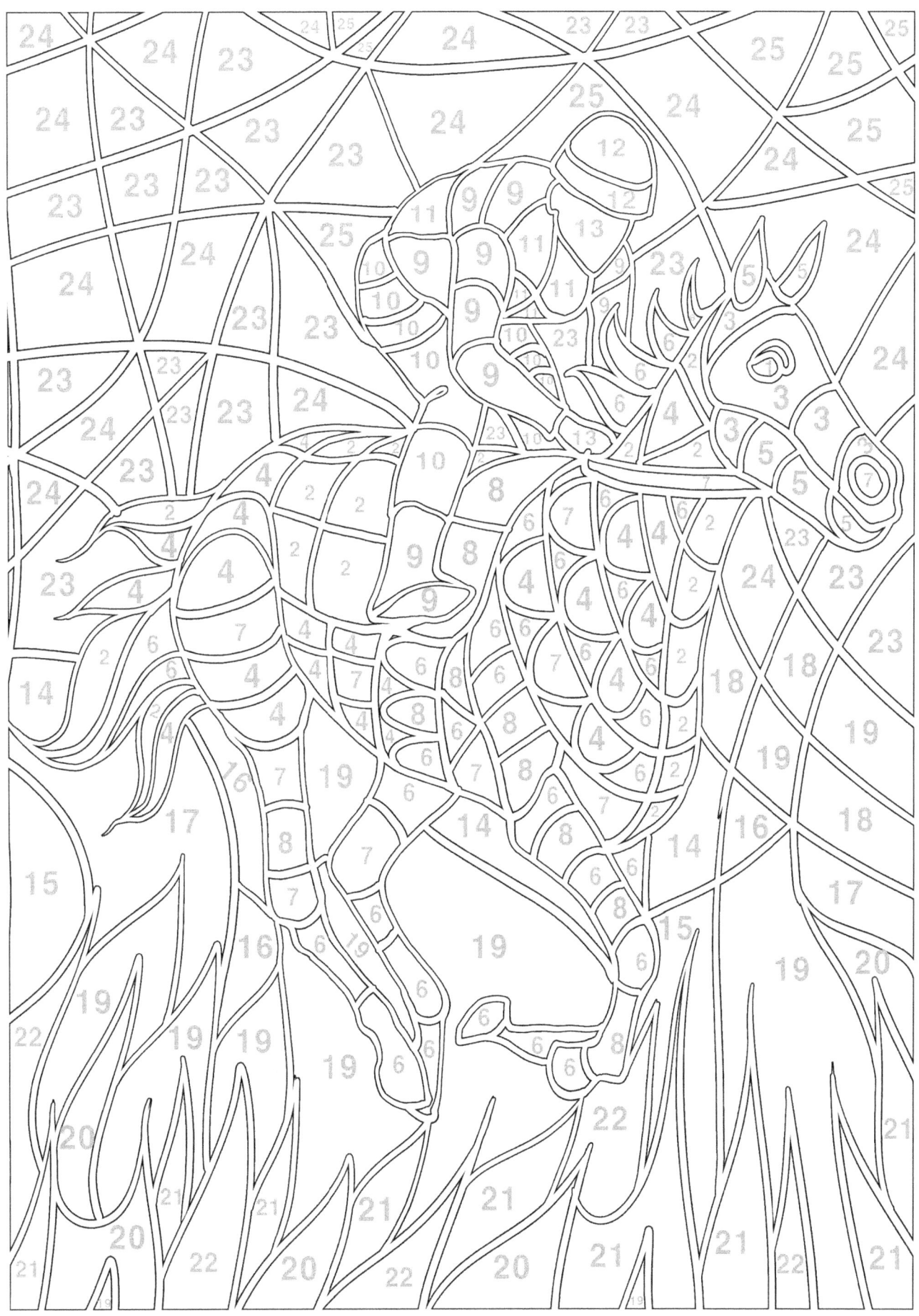

ENJOY BONUS
IMAGES FROM SOME
OF OUR
OTHER FUN
COLOR BY NUMBER
BOOKS!

FIND ALL OF OUR
BOOKS
ON AMAZON

Easy Design
Adult Color By Number
Jumbo Coloring Book of Large Print
Flowers, Birds, and Butterflies

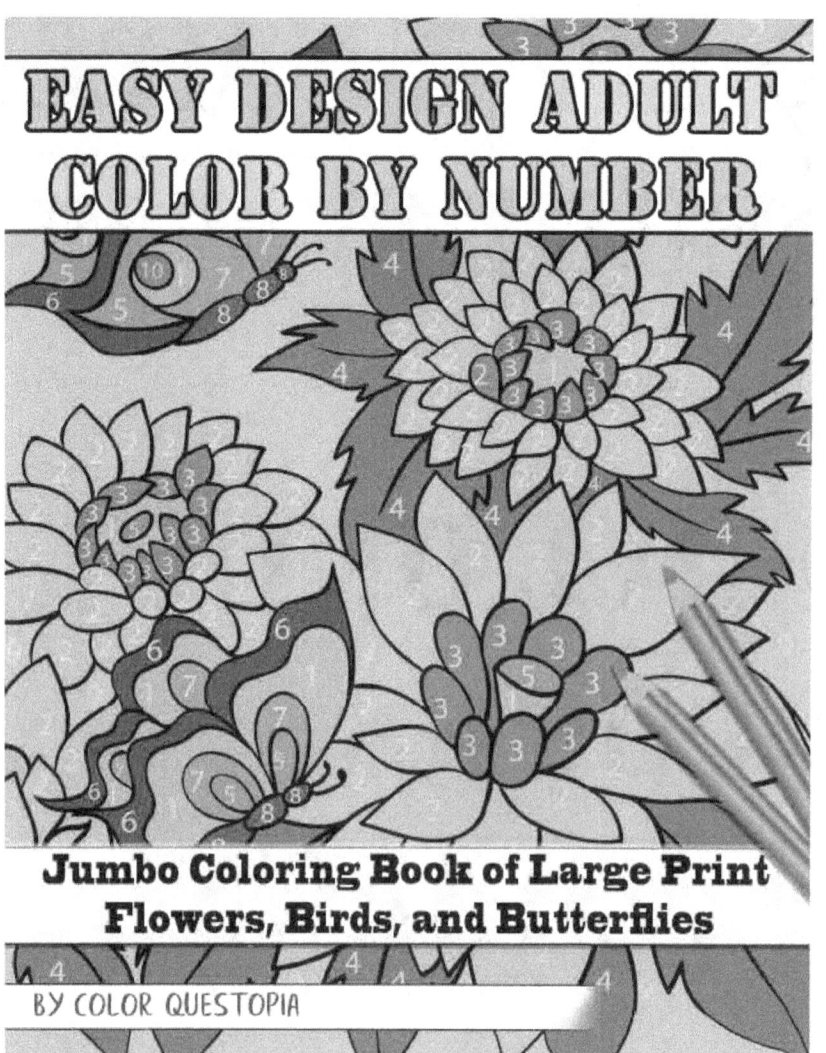

1. Red   2. Light Pink   3. Pink   4. Dark Green   5.Sky Blue   6. Brown
7. Dark Pink   8. Yellow   9. Green

New York
Mosaic Color by Number
Coloring Book for Adults

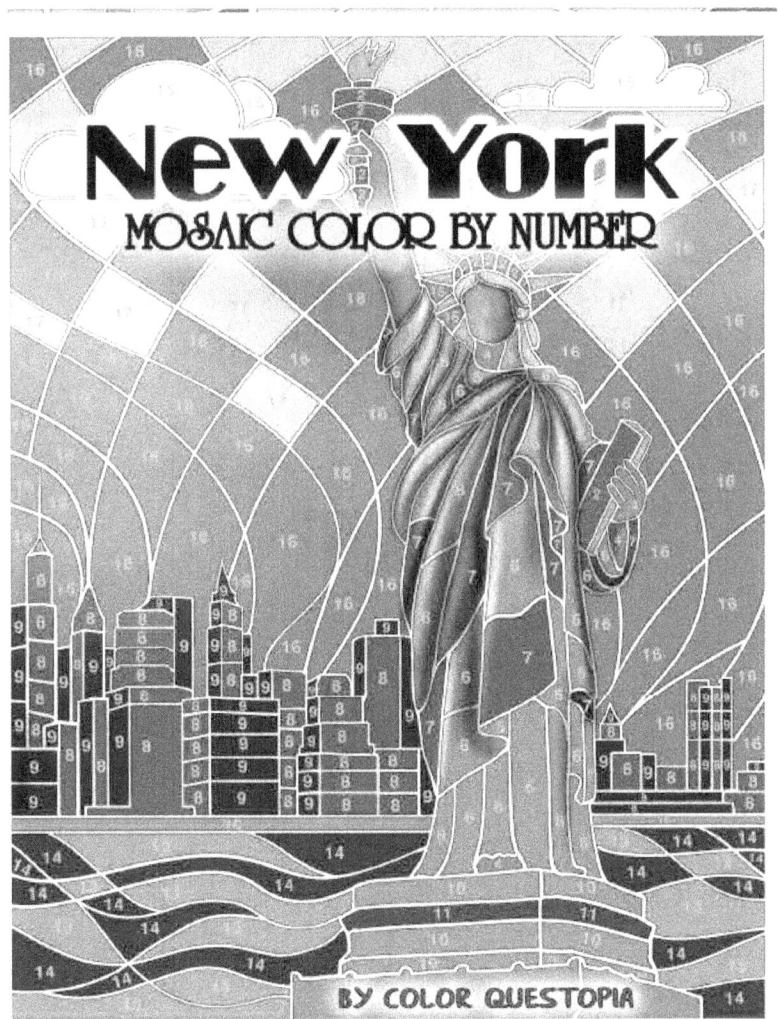

1. Yellow

2. Light Yellow

3. Dark Orange

4. Orange

5. Light Brown

6. Brown

7. Dark Brown

8. Light Red

9. Red

10. Violet

11. Light Violet

12. Light Orange

13. Dark Gray

14. Gray

15. Light Gray

16. Blue

17. Sky blue

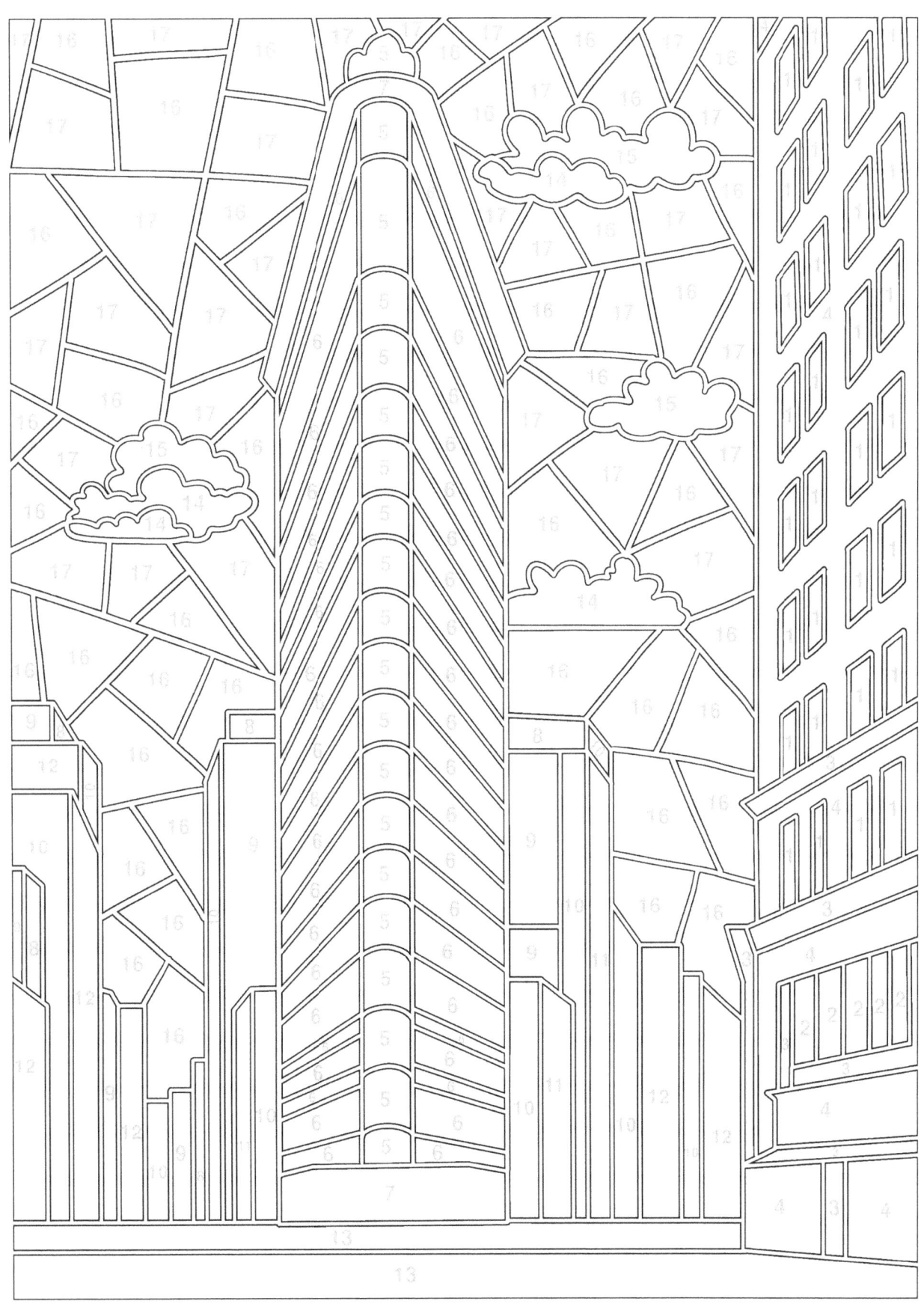

Country Farm Scenes
Nature, Animal, and Easy Designs
Adult Coloring Book
Color By Number For Adults

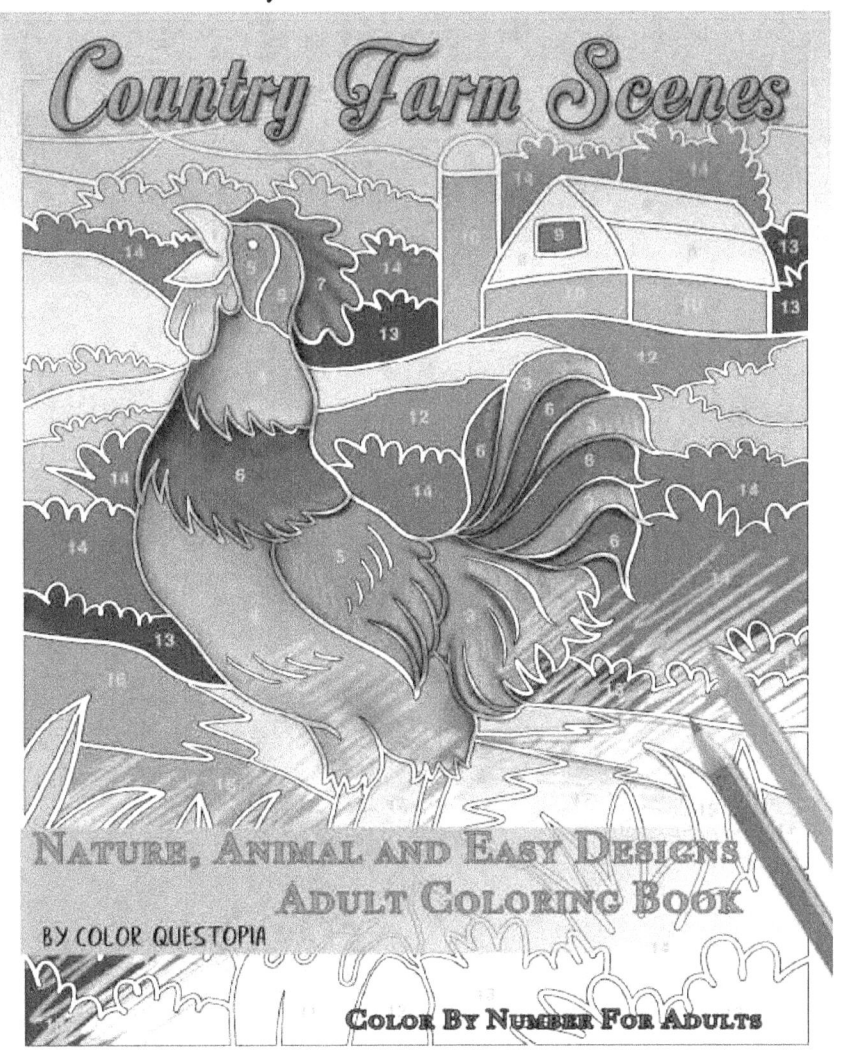

1. Black	16. Light pink
2. Reddish Brown	17. Pink
3. Dark Brown	18. Royal Blue
4. Light Brown	
5. Golden Yellow	
6. Orange	
7. Red	
8. Dark Yellow	
9. Light Yellow	
10. Beige	
11. Sky Blue	
12. Medium Blue	
13. Light Green	
14. Medium Green	
15. Dark Green	

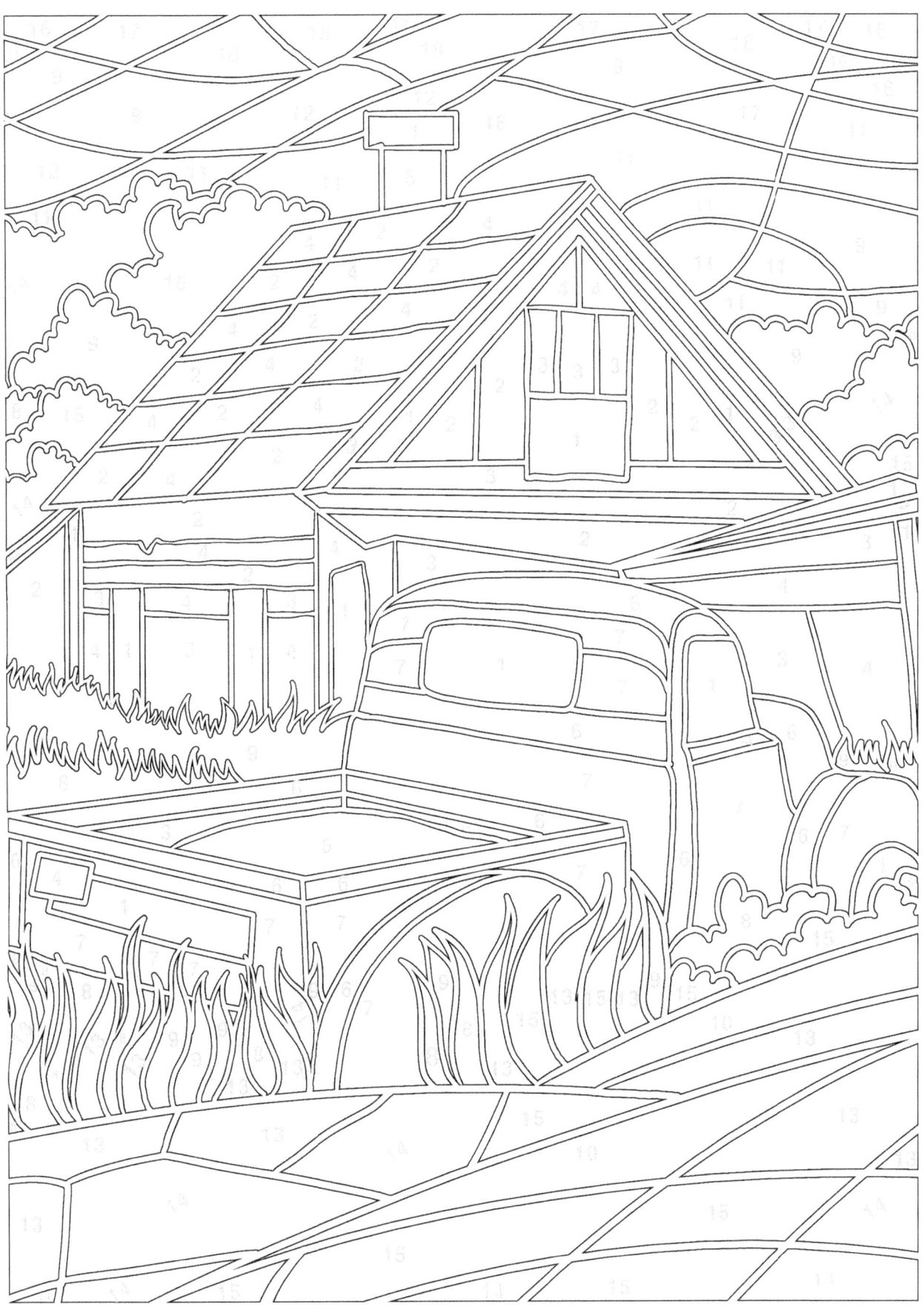

Fanciful Fox
Mosaic Adult Color by Number Book
Adult Coloring Book for Stress Relief
and Relaxation

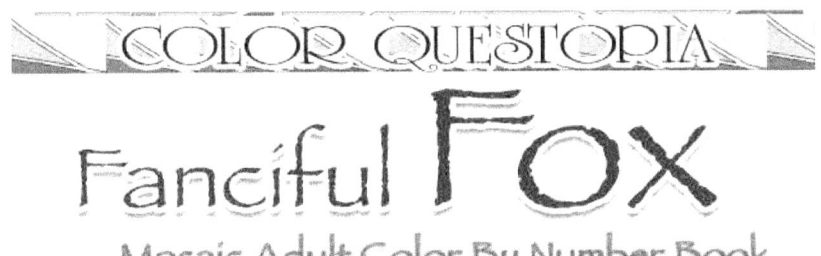

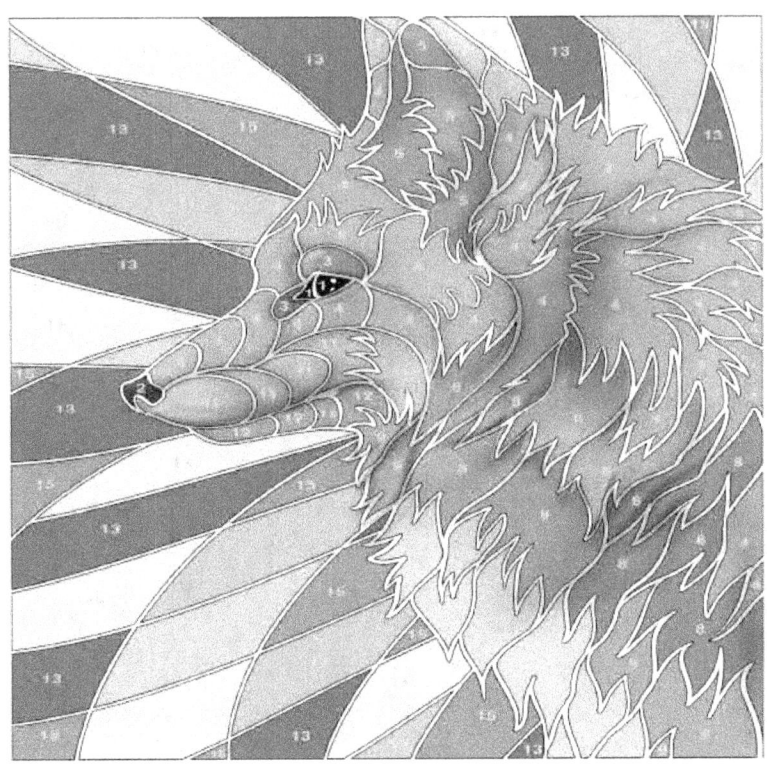

1. Black

2. Dark Brown

3. Light Red

4. Yellow

5. Medium Yellow

6. Medium Orange

7. Light Yellow

8. Brown

9. Light Orange

10. Orange

11. Light Brown

12. Dark Yellow

13. Dark Gray

14. Light Gray

15. Green

16. Light Green

17. Sky Blue

18. Blue

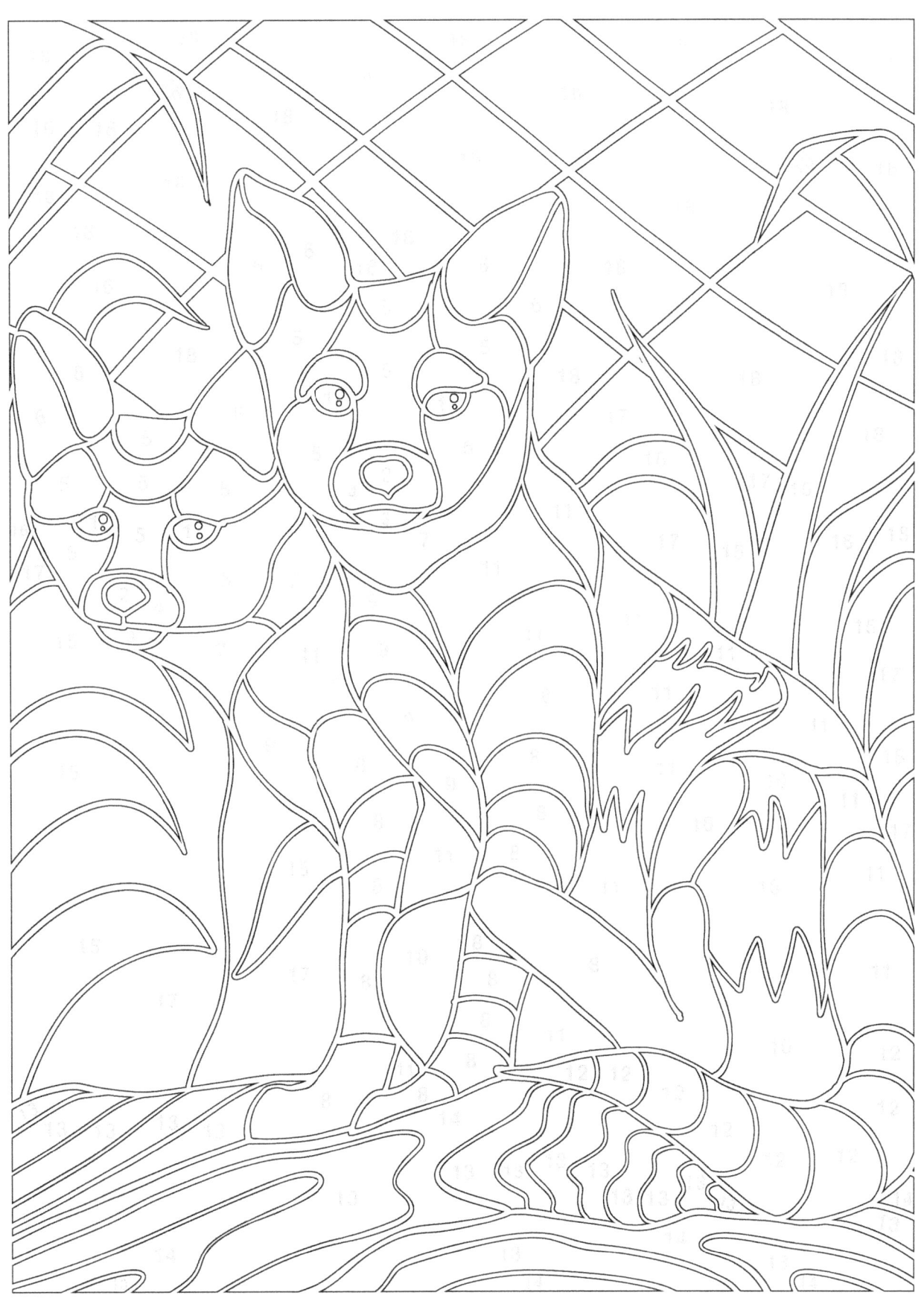

Beautiful Cities and Landmarks
Color by Number
Mosaic World Geography
Coloring Book For Adults

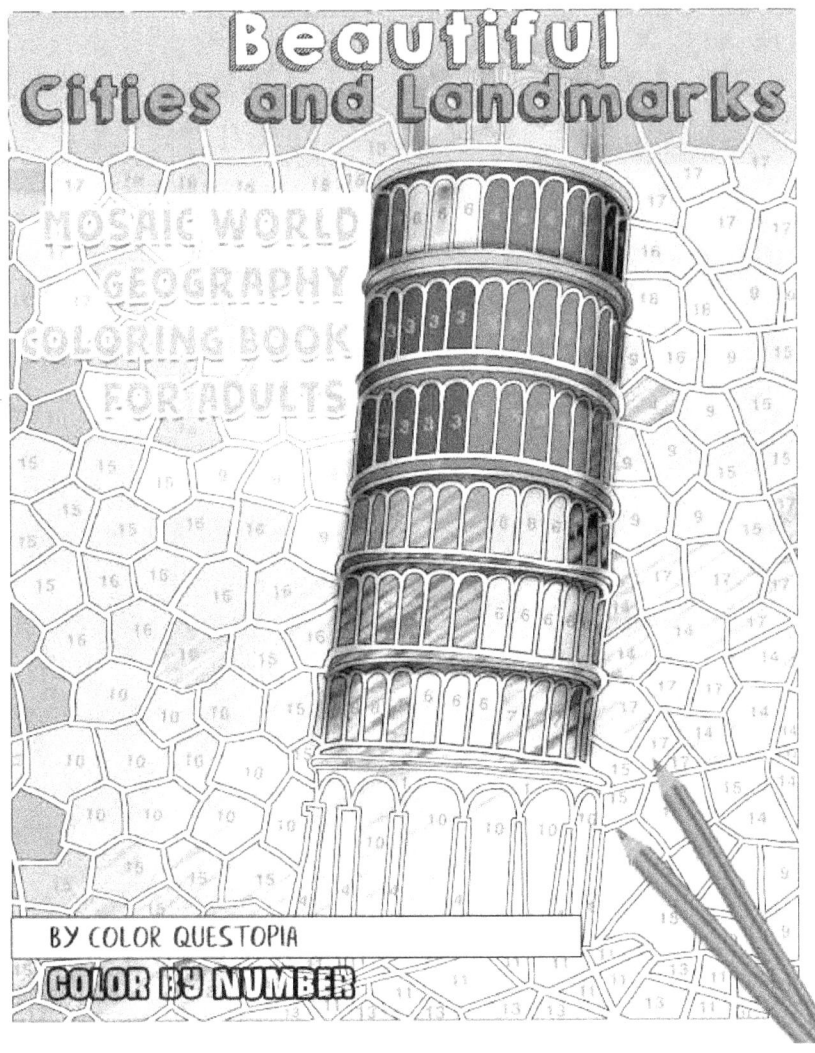

1. Light Gray	16. Orange
2. Dark Gray	17. Light Violet
3. Medium Gray	18. Yellow
4. Light Blue	19. Sky Blue
5. Gray	
6. Light Brown	
7. Brown	
8. Dark Brown	
9. Deep Green	
10. Light Green	
11. Neon Green	
12. Light Yellow	
13. Blue	
14. Light Blue	
15. Light Pink	

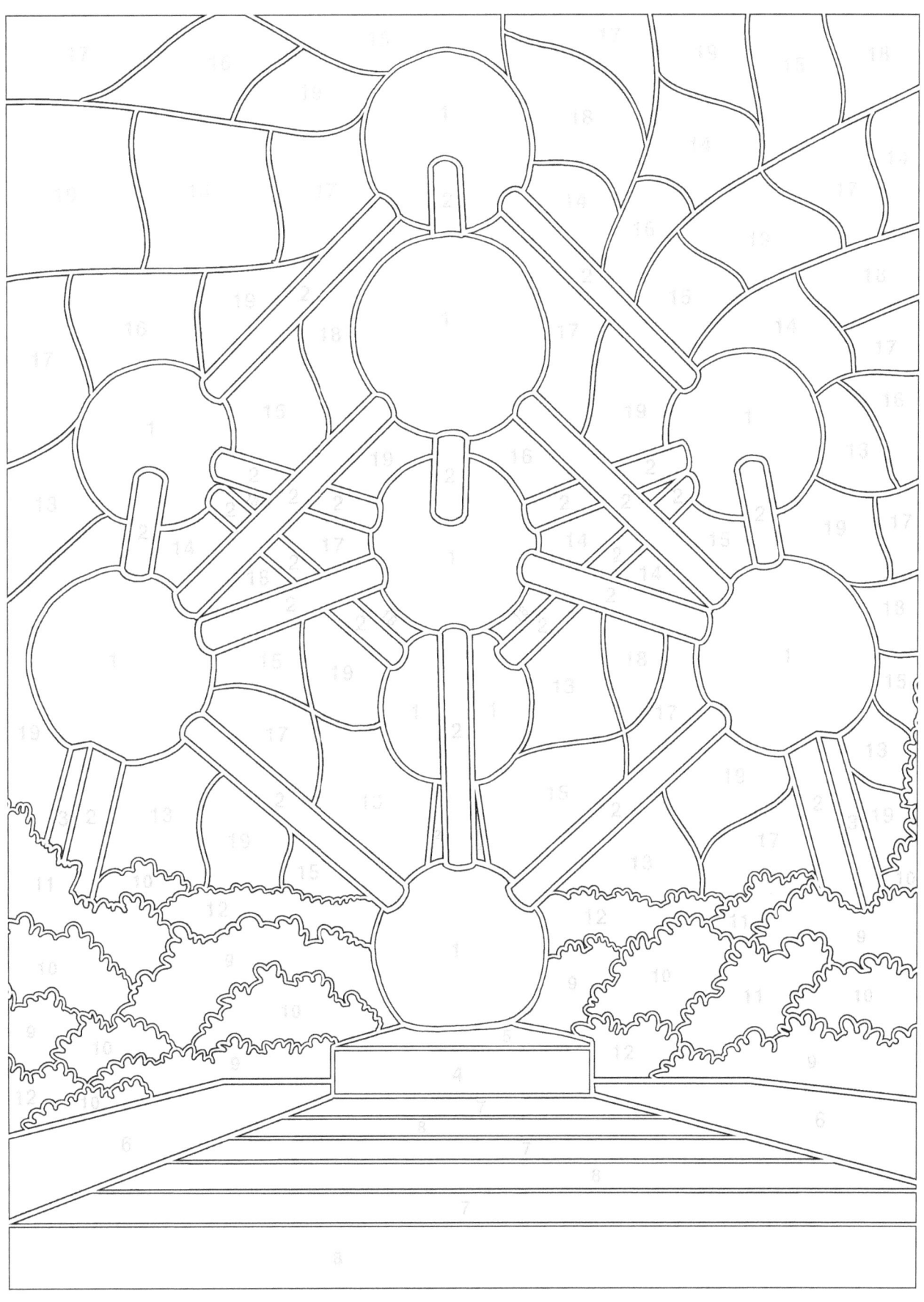

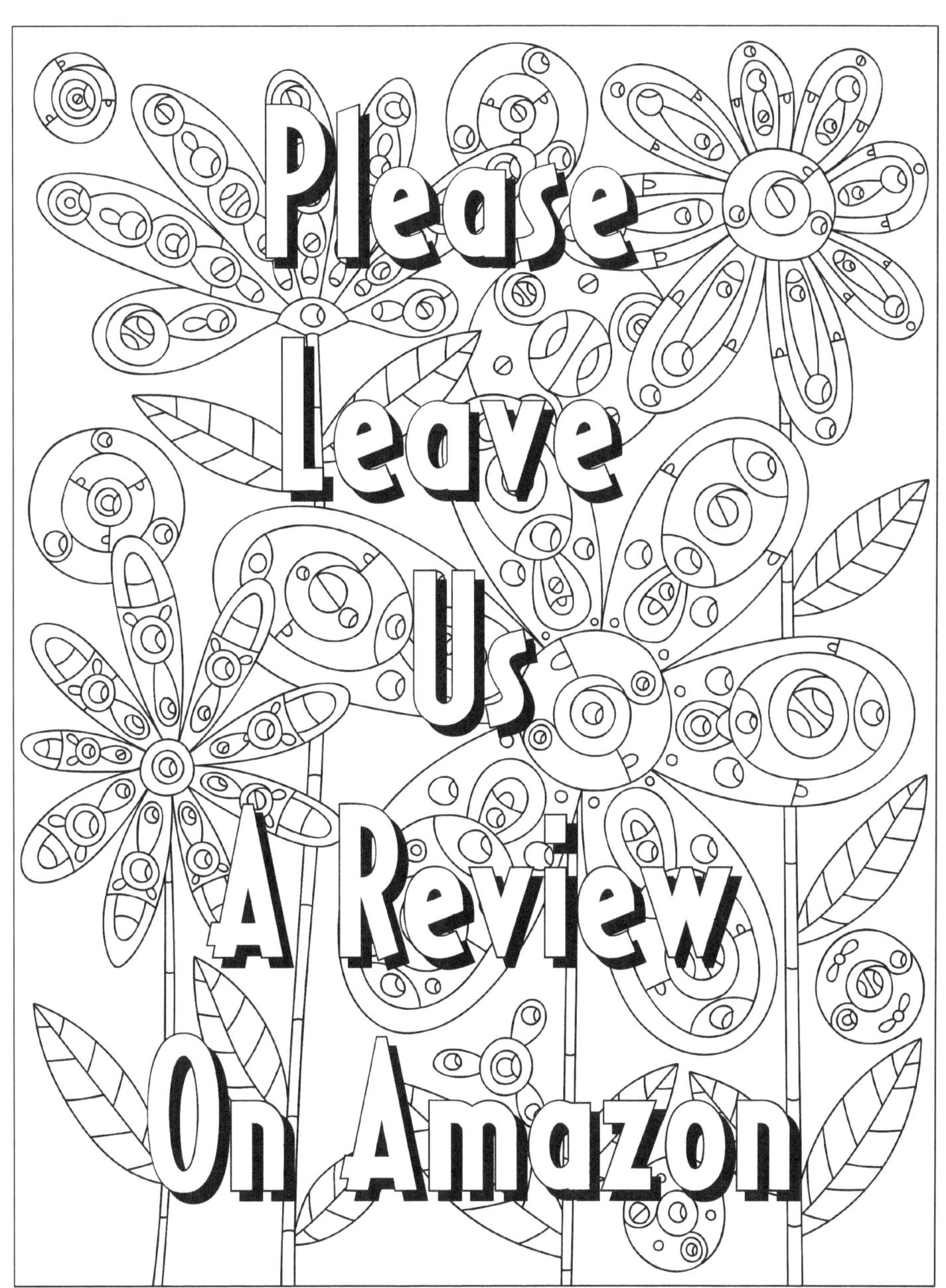

www.ingramcontent.com/pod-product-compliance
Lightning Source LLC
Chambersburg PA
CBHW080900220526
45467CB00008B/2582